Yas

W9-BBG-860

DO NOT REMOVE
CARDS FROM POCKET

THE IMPORTANCE OF

Christopher Columbus

by
Daniel C. Scavone

Lucent Books, P.O. Box 289011, San Diego, CA 92198-9011

To Cara

Acknowledgments

I wish to thank my university, the University of Southern Indiana, for generous support in the acquisition of the many resources needed for the creation of this volume. Thanks to the staff of the library, and especially to Ms. Gail Voteau for her incredible efficiency. Thanks to my wife Carolyn for the constancy of her encouragement and patience.

These and other titles are included in The Importance Of biography series:

Christopher Columbus	Chief Joseph
Marie Curie	Richard M. Nixon
Benjamin Franklin	Jackie Robinson
Galileo Galilei	H.G. Wells

Library of Congress Cataloging-in-Publication Data

Scavone, Daniel C., 1934–
    Christopher Columbus / Daniel C. Scavone.
        p. cm. — (The Importance of)
    Includes bibliographical references and index.
    Summary: A biography of explorer Christopher Columbus, from his early life, to his voyages, to his mixed legacy.
    ISBN 1-56006-034-4 (alk. paper)
    1. Columbus, Christopher—Juvenile literature. 2. Explorers–America–Biography–Juvenile literature. 3. Explorers–Spain–Biography–Juvenile literature. 4. America–Discovery and exploration–Spanish–Juvenile literature. [1. Columbus, Christopher. 2. Explorers.]   I. Title.   II. Series.
E111.S3   1992
970.01'5'092–dc20
    [B]   92-29499
                                                              CIP
                                                               AC

Contents

Foreword   5
Important Dates in the Life of Christopher
    Columbus   6

INTRODUCTION
Toward a Balanced View of Columbus   7

CHAPTER 1
Columbus: Early Life   9

CHAPTER 2
The Age of Columbus: Europe in 1492   21

CHAPTER 3
The First Voyage   31

CHAPTER 4
The Second Voyage   48

CHAPTER 5
Columbus's Last Voyages   62

CHAPTER 6
The Mixed Legacy of Christopher Columbus   76

Notes   89
For Further Reading   90
Works Consulted   92
Index   93
Picture Credits   96
About the Author   96

Foreword

THE IMPORTANCE OF biography series deals with individuals who have made a unique contribution to history. The editors of the series have deliberately chosen to cast a wide net and include people from all fields of endeavor. Individuals from politics, music, art, literature, philosophy, science, sports, and religion are all represented. In addition, the editors did not restrict the series to individuals whose accomplishments have helped change the course of history. Of necessity, this criterion would have eliminated many whose contribution was great, though limited. Charles Darwin, for example, was responsible for radically altering the scientific view of the natural history of the world. His achievements continue to impact the study of science today. Others, such as Chief Joseph of the Nez Percé, played a pivotal role in the history of their own people. While Joseph's influence does not extend much beyond the Nez Percé, his nonviolent resistance to white expansion and his continuing role in protecting his tribe and his homeland remain an inspiration to all.

These biographies are more than factual chronicles. Each volume attempts to emphasize an individual's contributions both in his or her own time and for posterity. For example, the voyages of Christopher Columbus opened the way to European colonization of the New World. Unquestionably, his encounter with the New World brought monumental changes to both Europe and the Americas in his day. Today, however, the broader impact of Columbus's voyages is being critically scrutinized. *Christopher Columbus,* as well as every biography in The Importance Of series, includes and evaluates the most recent scholarship available on each subject.

Each author includes a wide variety of primary and secondary source quotations to document and substantiate his or her work. All quotes are footnoted to show readers exactly how and where biographers derive their information, as well as provide stepping stones to further research. These quotations enliven the text by giving readers eyewitness views of the life and times of each individual covered in The Importance Of series.

Finally, each volume is enhanced by photographs, bibliographies, chronologies, and comprehensive indexes. For both the casual reader and the student engaged in research, The Importance Of biographies will be a fascinating adventure into the lives of people who have helped shape humanity's past, present, and will continue to shape its future.

Important Dates in the Life of Christopher Columbus

Born in Genoa, Italy.	1451	
Marries Doña Felipa Moniz Perestrello.	1476– 1478	Works as a map maker and bookseller. Makes several commercial voyages on Portuguese and Genoese ships.
Son Diego is born.	1480	
Works as a ship hand on Portuguese ships traveling to Guinea, Africa.	1482– 1485	Idea to reach the Indies by crossing the Atlantic is rejected by the Portuguese government. Moves with his son Diego to Spain.
Years of waiting for Spanish support for his voyage.	1484	Meets with Ferdinand and Isabella.
	1485– 1492	
Return voyage; leaves on second voyage; finds La Navidad destroyed and the men massacred. Founds Isabela.	1486	Son Fernando is born to Beatríz Enríquez de Arana. Again appeals to the king of Portugal, but Dias rounds Africa and ends Columbus's hopes in Portugal.
	1488	
Explores Cuba and Jamaica. Returns to find rebellion and wars in Hispaniola.	1492 1493 1494	Granada is defeated and the Spanish rulers decide to fund Columbus's voyage. Departs from Palos with three ships, and arrives in the Bahamas, on Guanahaní Island, renamed San Salvador. Discovers Cuba and Hispaniola, and founds La Navidad.
Returns to Cadiz, Spain.	1496	
Third voyage via Cape Verde Islands. Explores the northern coast of South America.	1498	
	1500	
Departs on fourth voyage.	1502	Columbus is arrested and leaves the colonies in chains. Received with honor by the king and queen of Spain.
Exploration of Central America; Heavy weather blows Columbus to Jamaica.	1502– 1503	
	1503– 1504	
Marooned on Jamaica.	1504	Last voyage home. Queen Isabella dies.
Ferdinand begins to revoke his contract with Columbus.	1505	
	1506	Columbus dies in Valladolid.

Toward a Balanced View of Columbus

In 1992, during the five-hundredth anniversary of Christopher Columbus's first voyage to America, Columbus's importance in history underwent a major reevaluation. Before 1992, history textbooks depicted Columbus's voyages from a very limited European point of view. Columbus was praised because his voyages led to Europe's discovery and settlement of the New World—and to the eventual founding of the United States of America in 1776. Most Americans viewed Columbus as possessing all the virtues that made the nation great: self-confidence, the courage of his convictions, wisdom, and most of all, the virtue of success.

But this interpretation left out people severely affected by Columbus's discovery, the native Americans, who had occupied the New World for 25,000 years. In 1992 the native Americans' side of history was emphasized. From the native American perspective, Columbus did not discover a "new world." Instead, he invaded and conquered a world they called home. Native Americans saw their people slaughtered

Native Americans viewed Columbus's "discovery" of America as an invasion.

Columbus's voyages had positive and negative consequences. Both should be examined when people consider his legacy.

and destroyed by white encroachment and diseases such as smallpox, which caused the extinction of whole nations of native American people.

Blacks, too, were victimized as a result of Columbus's arrival. Because the native American populations were devastated, white Europeans eventually sought the labor they needed from Africa, enslaving at least ten million black Africans.

Native Americans and black Americans thus have little to celebrate on Columbus Day. They, along with many white supporters, have struggled, using protests and writings, to change the way people think about Columbus and his legacy. Due largely to their efforts, Columbus has fallen from hero to villain among many Americans.

Many people argue that this interpretation, too, must be questioned, since much good also came of Columbus's achievement. Although not the first European to reach the New World, he did make the first transatlantic voyage to be fully recorded and to have lasting impact. In his time, crossing the vast uncharted ocean and leaving behind everything that was familiar and safe was as great a test of bravery and science as the manned space launchings were in the 1960s. Historian Daniel Boorstin has noted: "The long-past Age of Sail has taken away with it the wonder we should feel for Columbus's mastery of the winds," for he knew "how to harness the winds to carry him there and back."[1]

Yet it seems just as impossible to return to the view of Columbus as righteous hero. It is possible, however, to recognize and understand the good and the bad effects of Christopher Columbus's voyages. The year 1492 remains one of the great pivotal years in all of history. It serves as a dividing line between early and modern times. Prior to that crucial year, Africa, Asia, and Europe lay in absolute ignorance of the Americas, and the Americas lay isolated and insulated by two oceans; 1492 marked the modest beginnings of domination of the New World by the Old World.

Any new discussion of Columbus must attempt to find a balance between the two opposing perspectives: to recognize Columbus's contributions, but also to remember the repression and destruction of native American culture and beliefs.

1 Columbus: Early Life

Little is known about Christopher Columbus's early life. Scholars know that he was born in Genoa, Italy, in the year 1451. He was the oldest child of Domenico Columbus, wool weaver and tavern owner, and Susanna Fontanarossa. Christopher had two younger brothers, Bartolomé and Diego, and a sister, Bianchinetta.

As a child, Christopher received little formal education. Because he never wrote in the Tuscan Italian taught in schools, scholars assume that when he left Genoa he was only semiliterate. Most of his writings were in imperfect Spanish.

Biographers generally believe that young Columbus's education came mainly from the sailors who populated Genoa, a wealthy maritime commercial center. Genoa's people depended on the sea for their livelihood. Its fleet, along with that of Venice, Italy, sailed to Middle Eastern ports and carried back spices such as cinnamon and pepper, silks, and valuable gems. Like most Genoese boys, Christopher signed on for shipboard jobs whenever he could and made voyages to the Greek island of Chios, which then belonged to Genoa. During this time he probably learned some astronomy,

Christopher Columbus spent his early life learning the rudiments of sailing in the coastal city of Genoa.

Latin, and mathematics from fellow sailors. In addition, Columbus had a great natural intelligence and taught himself how to use navigational devices such as astrolabes, quadrants, and compasses.

Columbus in Portugal

In 1476, at twenty-five years of age, Columbus left Genoa for good and went to Portugal. Columbus's brother Bartolomé was already in Portugal working as a map maker, and Christopher may have worked with him for a time. The future explorer was already able to teach Bartolomé a great deal about maps, and Columbus, too, gathered much new geographical information by making accurate copies of seamen's maps. Many biographers believe that Columbus may also have worked as a bookseller in Lisbon and accumulated his personal library of geography books at this time.

Biographers know that Columbus read these geography books thoughtfully. Many remain today and they are filled with numerous notes in the margins. Because the bulk of his reading was done without teachers as guides, however, Columbus obtained many ideas that were clearly ridiculous. This helps to explain some of the farfetched ideas Columbus wrote about in his later journals and letters, such as his belief that he had discovered the Garden of Eden on his third voyage.

Columbus grew restless on land and frequently left Portugal to make several trips to Guinea. He described these voyages in his notes:

Under the equator, where the days are twelve hours long, lies the fortress of

During his youth, Columbus worked as a crewman on ships sailing to the Greek island of Chios and taught himself how to use navigational devices.

the Most Serene King of Portugal, which I visited. And I found the climate temperate. . . . When sailing from Lisbon to Guinea I made careful study of the course we followed, as pilots and mariners do. And later I took the altitude of the sun with quadrants and other instruments many times, and I found them to agree with Alfraganus [the tenth-century Arab geographer al-Farghani], that is, that there are 56⅔ miles per degree. Thus we may assert the circumference of earth at the equator to be 20,400 miles, or 5,100 leagues. And that is the truth.[2]

Columbus Marries

In Lisbon, in 1478 or 1479, Columbus married a Portuguese woman named Doña Felipa Moniz Perestrello. She was the daughter of a former Portuguese governor of the Madeiras island of Porto Santo, where the couple resided for a time. Their son Diego was born in 1480. Scholars think that Felipa may have died in childbirth, for neither Columbus nor Fernando, his son born seven years later to another woman, mentioned her in their subsequent writings.

About this time Columbus began to become obsessed with reaching the Indies (present-day India) by sailing west across

An Enemy of Swearing and Blasphemy

Fernando provides a son's view of Columbus in this excerpt from The Life of Christopher Columbus by His Son Ferdinand.

"The Admiral was a well-built man of more than average stature, the face long, the cheeks somewhat high, his body neither fat nor lean. He had an aquiline nose and light-colored eyes; his complexion too was light and tending to bright red. In youth his hair was blonde, but when he reached the age of thirty, it all turned white. In eating and drinking, and in the adornment of his person, he was very moderate and modest. He was affable in conversation with strangers and very pleasant to the members of his household, though with a certain gravity. He was so strict in matters of religion that for fasting and saying prayers he might have been taken for a member of a religious order. He was so great an enemy of swearing and blasphemy that I give my word I never heard him utter any other oath than 'by St. Ferdinand!' and when he grew very angry with someone, his rebuke was to say 'God take you!' for doing or saying that."

Columbus strictly followed the rules of the Catholic church.

Columbus explains his theory of a westward route to the Indies.

the Atlantic. This idea was still unclear in his mind in 1481—more a dream than a plan—but over the next ten years he became ever more confident that it could be done. At the time Columbus knew many others were attempting to find a way to the Indies, and so he was in a hurry to find a sponsor for his voyage before someone else found the route. All of Europe was searching for this route since the Turks had captured Constantinople in 1453. The Moslems of the Ottoman Turkish Empire controlled both the land and sea routes to India. Genoese and Venetian ships still carried goods from Asia back to Europe, but the Moslems were charging exorbitant port fees and duties. Europe sorely needed a route to India that avoided Turkish ports. Columbus knew that the first man to find such a route would immediately gain fame and fortune.

Because Portugal was located on the western edge of Europe, bordering on the Atlantic Ocean, it was far ahead of the rest of Europe in exploring the route to the Indies, and the Portuguese had been sailing south down the African coast, hoping to find an eastern passage to the Indies. In 1484 Columbus first sought the support of the king of Portugal, John II, for his ideas, because of Portugal's interest.

When Columbus met with John II's advisors, he argued that the Atlantic was narrow, and that Asia was large and wrapped around the globe, reaching far into the Atlantic, very near Europe. He claimed he could reach the easternmost edge of Asia, the islands of Cipango (now Japan) by sailing west. He estimated the journey to be under 3,000 miles. The king's advisors were not convinced and advised King John II against advancing Columbus any money. We know today that they were right, since the actual distance west from Europe to Japan is more like 10,000 miles.

Columbus in Spain

In 1485, after this failure, Columbus left Portugal with Diego, age three, to present his idea to the Spanish rulers, Queen Isabella and King Ferdinand. In Spain

Columbus left Diego in the care of the Franciscans at La Rabida monastery near Palos, on the southwest coast. Then he began his quest to find someone who had access to the king and queen to recommend him and what he called his Enterprise of the Indies to the royal couple. Columbus spent the years from 1485 to 1492 in this venture, and they were seven of the most crucial and frustrating years of his life.

The first person to aid and support Columbus in gaining an audience with the Spanish royal couple was Friar Antonio de Marchena, an astronomer-monk known to the king and queen. Friar Marchena went to Madrid to personally support Columbus's ideas before the king and queen.

In response to Friar Marchena's request, the monarchs invited Columbus to the royal court at Córdoba in January 1486. While awaiting their arrival, Columbus

Early Ideas on Reaching the Indies

In The Life of Christopher Columbus, *Fernando talks about his father's marriage and early thoughts about sailing west to the Indies.*

"A lady named Doña Felipa Moniz Perestrello, of noble birth, . . . became his wife. . . . They went to live with [her mother] who, observing the Admiral's great interest in geography, told him . . . her husband had been a notable seafarer. . . . Seeing that her stories of these voyages gave the Admiral much pleasure, she gave him the writings and sea-charts left by her husband. These things excited the Admiral still more; and he informed himself of the other voyages and navigations that the Portuguese were then making to Mina and down the Coast of Guinea, and greatly enjoyed speaking with the men who sailed in those regions. . . . The Admiral while in Portugal began to speculate that if the Portuguese could sail so far south, it should be possible to sail as far westward, and that it was logical to expect to find land in that direction.

To obtain confirmation on this point, he turned anew to study the writers on geography with whose work he was already familiar, and to consider the astronomical arguments that might support his design; consequently, he noted down any helpful hints that sailors or other persons might drop. He made such good use of all these things that he grew convinced beyond the shadow of a doubt that to the west of the Canary and Cape Verde Islands lay many lands which could be reached and discovered."

The Talavera Commission

Fernando's biography of Columbus describes his father's frustrating interviews with the Talavera commission set up by Ferdinand and Isabella to judge his plan to sail west.

"As there were not so many geographers then as now, the members of this committee were not so well informed as the business required. Nor did the Admiral wish to reveal all the details of his plan, fearing lest it be stolen from him in Castile as it had been in Portugal. . . . Some [committee members] argued: In all the thousands of years since God created the world, those lands had remained unknown to innumerable learned men and experts in navigation; and it was most unlikely that the Admiral should know more than all other men, past and present. Others, who based themselves on geography, claimed the world was so large that to reach the end of Asia . . . would take more than three years. . . . They questioned whether habitable lands existed at the other end. . . . Others argued . . . that if one were to set out, . . . one would not be able to return to Spain because the world was round. . . . For that would be like sailing a ship [uphill] to the top of a mountain: a thing that ships could not do even with the aid of the strongest wind.

The Admiral gave suitable replies to all these objections. In the end, they condemned the enterprise as vain and impossible."

Columbus speaks before the royal court of Spain.

Friar Pérez blesses the kneeling Columbus. The priest presented Columbus's ideas to the king and queen of Spain.

lived in the house of the royal treasurer, Alfonso de Quintanilla. The sovereigns arrived in Córdoba in April, and Columbus had his first audience in May.

The monarchs were impressed enough by Columbus's plan to order a royal panel of scholars and mariners to study its feasibility. They even provided living expenses for Columbus until a decision could be reached. The first meetings were held in the north-central Spanish city of Salamanca so that scholars of the city's university could be present. Columbus pleaded his case before this group of experts from November 1486 to January 1487. He explained why he believed that the Atlantic was narrow. He showed them the writings of the ancient Greek geographers and passages in Marco Polo's journal that indicated the chances of reaching Cipango were quite good. After months of consideration, however, the commission advised Ferdinand and Isabella in August to reject Columbus's proposal.

Despite this decision, Isabella informed Columbus that they would again consider his ideas, but there were more important matters to take care of at the moment. Spain was in the midst of its attempts to capture the Moslem fortress of Granada in southern Spain, which was already under attack and required all the country's attention. The siege of Granada became the final act of the long series of Spanish wars in which Spanish Christians won control of Spain from Spanish Moslems in an attempt to reunite the country under a single Christian rule. This crusade was known as the Reconquista (Reconquest) and began in the eleventh century. By 1105 the Spanish city of Toledo had been retaken; by 1250 Córdoba and all other Moslem strongholds in Spain had fallen as well. At the time Columbus approached Ferdinand and Isabella, only Granada in the extreme south of the peninsula remained under Moslem control.

Isabella told Columbus that when all of Spain was Catholic and united under their rule, the monarchs would have the leisure and the funds to begin thinking about other matters. Columbus may not have been as encouraged by this if he had known that the war would drag on for four more long years.

Columbus waited. From October of 1487, when his royal expense account ended, to March 1488, he again worked as a map maker and bookseller in Córdoba and Seville. He read everything he could find on the subject of geography during this period and made marginal notes in his own books. He lived with his mistress, Beatríz Enríquez de Arana, during these months, and in 1488 she bore him a son, Fernando. The longer Columbus waited, the more frustrated he became. He knew that Portugal was waging a relentless effort

Columbus estimated that the westward distance between Europe and present-day Japan was 3,000 miles. In fact, the distance is 10,000 miles.

to sail down the west coast of Africa to find a direct eastern route by sea to India. Portuguese expeditions inched their way farther down the coast each year but had still not turned the corner of southern Africa. That immense continent extended farther to the south than anyone had ever suspected.

In 1488 Columbus again wrote to King John of Portugal. The king was responsive, and on March 20 he invited Columbus to come to Portugal. Columbus and his brother Bartolomé arrived in Lisbon in December 1488. Unfortunately, at this very time, Bartholomeu Dias and his three *caravels* (small, light sailing ships) triumphantly sailed up the Tagus River from the Atlantic to Lisbon with the news that they had rounded the Cape of Good Hope. This news crushed Columbus's efforts to obtain funds from Portugal for a westward voyage across the Atlantic to the Indies. Dias had just opened the shortest way to India by sailing directly east.

Bartholomeu Dias discovered an eastward route from Europe to India by sailing three caravels around the Cape of Good Hope.

Isabella's Decision

Fernando's biography describes the following crucial episode between Queen Isabella and Luis de Santángel, her state treasurer.

"On the same day that the Admiral departed [to gain French support in January 1492] . . . Luis de Santángel . . . told the Queen he was surprised that her Highness . . . should [refuse] an enterprise that offered so little risk yet could prove of so great service to God and the exaltation of His Church, not to speak of the very great increase and glory of her realms and kingdoms. . . . Moreover, if any other ruler should [sponsor Columbus] it would clearly be a great injury to her estate. . . . Since the . . . Admiral . . . sought to take his reward only from what he found, and was ready not only to venture his person but to contribute a part of the costs, the Sovereigns . . . would be regarded as generous and highminded princes for having tried to penetrate the secrets of the universe. Admitted the outcome was doubtful, . . . [Queen Isabella] should not let it be said that for fear of losing so small an amount she abandoned that enterprise.

The Catholic Queen, who knew Santángel's zeal in her service, thanked him for his good advice and said that she was even ready to pledge her jewels for the cost of the expedition. But Santángel . . . said this would not be necessary; he would be happy to render her Highness a trifling service by lending her the money. So, having made her decision, the Queen sent a court bailiff posthaste to order the Admiral to return."

Columbus meets with Queen Isabella.

Upon his return from Lisbon to Spain, Columbus resided in the house of the wealthy count of Medinaceli, whom he had met earlier, probably through Friar Marchena. The count was much interested in overseas shipping opportunities and believed in Columbus enough to urge him to approach Isabella again. The count even wrote to Isabella that he would personally finance the voyage, but he knew that such an ambitious and important project ought to have royal consent. This letter made a favorable impression on Isabella, and she again summoned Columbus—this time to the military base at Jaén in southern Spain in May 1489. The queen told Columbus that final victory over Granada seemed near, and with it would come Columbus's fleet. He remained in the royal camp until January 1490. But Granada held out, and Columbus became concerned that the monarchs would never fund his voyage.

Another year went by. Christopher and his son Diego went to seek funds from

Columbus's Contract

The official contract that contained the honors and powers granted to Columbus was entitled "Title Granted by the Catholic Sovereigns to Cristóbal Colon, Admiral, Viceroy and Governor of the Islands and Mainland That May Be Discovered." *Here is the key portion, from E. G. Bourne, ed.,* The Northmen, Columbus, and Cabot.

"Don Ferdinand and Donna Isabella, by the grace of God King and Queen of Castile, Leon, Aragon, Sicily, Granada, Toledo, Valencia, Sardinia, Cordova, Corsica, etc. Since you, Cristóbal Colon, are going by our command, with some of our ships and with our subjects, to discover and acquire certain islands and mainland in the ocean, . . . It is our will and pleasure that you . . . shall be our Admiral and Viceroy therein and shall be empowered to entitle yourself Don Cristóbal Colon, and that your sons and successors in said office shall likewise call themselves Don, Admiral, Viceroy, and Governor thereof. . . . forever and ever. . . . And you may have power to judge civil and criminal cases according to the law. . . . Given in our city of Granada on 30 April, in the year of the Nativity of our Lord Jesus Christ 1492. I the King. I the Queen."

In addition, the Articles of Agreement said:
"Item: that of all and every kind of merchandise, whether pearls, precious stones, gold, silver, spices, etc., . . . Don Cristóbal Colon shall take for himself one tenth after expenses. . . . Agreed. 17 April 1492."

King Charles VIII of France. Bartolomé had had some success in gaining the French king's interest in Columbus's ideas, but the abbot of La Rabida monastery, Friar Juan Pérez, persuaded Columbus to delay his trip. Pérez was on good terms with Queen Isabella and decided to write to her on Columbus's behalf.

Isabella received this letter in time to send messengers to intercept Columbus's departure from Spain and request that he come to Santa Fé, a town just below the fortress of Granada, from which she and her armies were conducting the ongoing siege. This time she even sent money for his trip. Columbus arrived, only to wait several more months.

Columbus Wins His Commission to Sail

On January 2, 1492, Granada surrendered, and Ferdinand and Isabella finally ended Columbus's seven-year ordeal of patience by listening carefully to his plan. In the final discussions Columbus asked for much in return for his personal risk. He demanded knighthood, the titles of Admiral and Viceroy (literally "substitute king") in all the islands and mainlands he should discover and payment of 10 percent of all gold and profits from spices—after expenses—for himself and his descendants forever. Titles and honors such as these would raise Columbus and his family to the ranks of Spanish nobility. They would assure his personal control and management of any gold or other valuable products he should discover.

Columbus was asking for a great deal, and the monarchs hesitated. But ultimately they consented to everything he demanded. They no doubt had many reasons for doing this. They may have felt the task was impossible and that there was very little risk involved on their part. On the outside chance that he did succeed, Columbus might return with so much wealth that their own 90 percent would still amount to a fortune. Also, Columbus was very persistent, and his religious convictions fit well with the devout queen's own. Columbus believed it was his divine mission to return with enough wealth to finance a new crusade to take Jerusalem away from the hated Turks.

These reasons played a part in persuading the Spanish government to gamble on Columbus. But one factor must have been paramount in the monarchs' decision: Columbus revealed an intimate knowledge of the prevailing winds he would encounter. He related to the monarchs that on trips to Guinea he had noted that ships sailing out from Spain and bound for the Canary Islands, seven hundred miles to the southwest, were soon aided by the northeasterly winds that blew out from Europe. Columbus told the king and queen that these winds were perfect, since he believed Cipango (Japan) was directly to the west, on the same latitude as the Canaries. And he was sure Cipango's offshore islands reached far into the Atlantic toward Europe.

This knowledge impressed Ferdinand and Isabella because ships attempting to sail directly west from Portugal into the Ocean Sea sailed into the teeth of the prevailing west winds, and they had always failed to get very far. Ships returning from the Canaries sailed straight north until they picked up these strong westerlies, which helped them easily reach Lisbon.

Columbus knew where and how to find winds that would take his ships across the Ocean Sea and winds that would bring them back home again.

Final Preparations Before Sailing

Once Columbus had his royal contract in hand, he turned his attention to fitting out ships and crew. By May 12, 1492, Columbus was in the southwestern Spanish seaport of Palos, where Martin Alonso Pinzón, one of the leading citizens of the town, assisted him in signing up skilled men and in locating dependable caravels. Both Martin Alonso Pinzón and his brother Vincente Yañez Pinzón were willing to help. Both had expressed similar dreams of finding India by sailing west.

The crown sent Columbus to Palos to equip his journey because the town owed the government the use of two caravels as a fine for breaking a law. In addition to the *Santa Maria,* a *nao* or *carrack* (galleon) type of ship, the town of Palos arranged for the use of two caravels, the *Niña* and the *Pinta.*

The *Santa Maria,* which would be the flagship, was a round-bellied craft. At 82 by 28 feet, carrying thirty-six men, she was larger than the two sleeker, faster caravels. They were about 60 by 20 feet, and each carried about twenty-five men. Because of the uncertainties about how far Columbus and his men had to journey and how long they would be at sea, they carried provisions for a whole year.

Columbus set his departure date for August 3. Biographer Björn Landström described the event:

Columbus was given a total of three ships: two caravels, the Niña *and the* Pinta; *and one carrack, the* Santa Maria.

During their last few days ashore, everyone had made his confession and taken the communion, and on the evening of August 2 the crews were called aboard. Columbus took the communion and was rowed out to his ship before dawn. Then, in the name of Jesus, he gave the order to set the sails and weigh anchor. There was half an hour to go before sunrise, and the cocks of Palos were not yet crowing. . . . The *Santa Maria,* the *Pinta,* and the *Niña* . . . sailed out in a freshening . . . wind.[3]

They would soon pick up the desired and expected northeasterly winds that would make the voyage a success.

These ships were destined to sail more than 3,000 miles. Columbus's men did not yet know that they would be beyond sight of any land for thirty-six seemingly endless days and nights. No sailors in known maritime history had so boldly challenged the unknown sea with its imagined monsters and its quite real dangers.

2 The Age of Columbus: Europe in 1492

In 1492 Columbus was not the first or the only mariner with the idea of sailing west to reach India. The events and ideas that shaped Columbus's thinking influenced other Europeans as well. It was a unique combination of the reemergence of important ideas on geography and travel, as well as a rekindling of interest in the world, that made Columbus's voyage possible. In the age of Columbus, Italy was in the midst of one of history's great golden ages. The Middle Ages of Europe (about 500 to 1300 A.D.) were over and a new era, one that Italian poets such as Petrarch called a Rinascimento or Rinascitá, a "Rebirth," had begun.

During this period, commonly known by the French term the Renaissance, many ancient Greek and Roman manuscripts that had been lost or forgotten were rediscovered in the niches and attics of monastery libraries. For centuries, during the Middle Ages when Christian Europe was dominated by religious authority, these books had gone unread. But in the spirit of discovery that dominated the Renaissance, these manuscripts became widely read.

People of the Renaissance found that these old manuscripts contained valuable information that could be applied to their own time. For example, the secrets of Roman builders, whose temples and roads were solidly made, were rediscovered in the book *On Architecture* by the Roman, Vitruvius.

The ancient Greek book of practical information that had the greatest influence on Columbus was Claudius Ptolemy's *Geography*. Claudius Ptolemy lived in Alexandria, Egypt (90–168 A.D.), during the Roman Empire. When *Geography* was rediscovered in 1410, it was immediately translated into Latin by Manuel Chrysoloras, a Greek scholar from Constantinople. Ptolemy's book presented a map with a complete system of latitudes and longitudes on which the locations of 8,000 places were plotted. Ptolemy's map also attempted to project the spherical world onto a flat surface. *Geography* became a starting point for modern *cartography* (the science of map making). It held a gold mine of information about the earth that had been forgotten during the Middle Ages. The impact of this information on the leaders and scholars of Columbus's time was tremendous. According to Daniel Boorstin, when *Geography* was rediscovered, "Not only for Columbus, but for the Arabs and others who had put their faith in classical learning, Ptolemy remained the source, the standard, and the sovereign of world geography."[4]

Ptolemy's map accurately revealed that he believed the earth was round. But the

The writings of Claudius Ptolemy provided Renaissance scholars with long lost information about the earth.

map also contained two errors. First it made the earth smaller, 23,625 miles in circumference, than it actually is (24,900 miles around the equator). Second and more importantly, it showed Africa, labeled Terra Incognita ("Unknown Lands") in the south, reaching far eastward to join with Asia and westward almost touching Europe at the Straits of Gibraltar. Thus a ring of continents enclosed the Mediterranean Sea, the Indian Ocean, and the China Sea in their center. According to this map, ships could never sail to the Far East, directly to Cathay, as China was then known.

These mistakes, the smaller earth and the impossibility of reaching Cathay by sailing east, encouraged Columbus westward. Once Columbus settled on this idea, he began to study astronomical arguments and other bits of information that supported it. When he found a source that

Columbus's Personal Library

Columbus's personal library consisted mainly of geography books, which he read time and again, and to which he added more than twenty-five hundred comments of his own in the margins. Kirkpatrick Sale enumerates Columbus's books:

"Seven of his personal volumes, most with extensive marginalia, . . . have survived and are preserved today in the Biblioteca Colombina in Seville. Three of the books are full of travelers' fancies and descriptions of monstrous beings: Marco Polo's *Orientalium regionum* [also known as *Marco Polo's Travels*] . . . Pierre d'Ailly's fanciful *Imago mundi* [*Shape of the World*] and other treatises (1480–83); and Pliny's classic *Historia naturalis* [*Natural History*] in Italian translation (1489). The others were Pope Pius II's *Historia rerum ubique gestarum* [*History of the World*] (1477) [and] Plutarch's *Lives*. . . . Fernando listed, in chapters 6 and 7 of his biography, a number of other sources he assumed his father read."

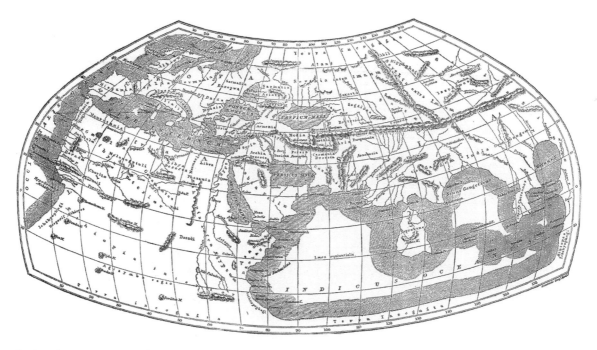

Ptolemy's map contained two errors: It depicted the earth as smaller than it actually is, and it incorrectly joined Africa with Asia.

verified his theory, such as an argument for a smaller globe or a larger Asia (thus a smaller Atlantic), he adopted it.

When he approached Isabella, Columbus used only the statistics most favorable to his enterprise. Columbus's intent was not to prove the world was round (most educated Europeans knew this), but to convince the queen that the Atlantic was smaller than people believed. He did this by lowering the number of degrees occupied by empty sea, by reducing the distance of a degree, and by proving that Ptolemy's circumference was too large. Columbus also argued that Asia was larger than thought, reaching nearer to Europe on its eastern edge.

Columbus reduced the size of the earth in his reckoning by basing his calculations on the work of a tenth-century Arab geographer named al-Farghani. Al-Farghani surmised that one degree of latitude at the equator measured 56⅔ miles. By multiplying 56⅔ miles by 360 (the number of degrees in a circle), Columbus believed he proved that the earth's circumference was 20,400 miles, 3,200 miles less than Ptolemy's calculations and 4,500 miles smaller than it is. Unfortunately, he did not know that al-Farghani's Arabic mile was actually 7,089 feet, one-and-one-third times larger than the 5,280-foot Roman mile used by the Western world. In reality, al-Farghani had determined the earth to be about 27,400 miles around—Columbus's 20,400 times 1⅓ (neither al-Farghani nor Columbus knew that a degree is really 69 Roman miles).

Marco Polo's Account of Cathay

No single book, however, fired the imagination of Europe and fueled Columbus's desire more than Marco Polo's account of his thirteenth-century travels in Cathay, and Columbus's personal copy of the book contained numerous comments in its margins. Marco Polo's report of his overland journeys throughout Asia greatly stimulated European interest in geography and in the size and shape of the earth. Polo spent seventeen years in the service of the Great Khan of Cathay, Kublai Khan, traveling on numerous missions of state. Knowing Kublai's great curiosity about other peoples and places, Marco took many notes so that he might please the khan with his reports. After an absence of twenty-four years, Marco returned to Venice in 1295.

Marco Polo's writings about China inspired Columbus to find a way to reach it by sea.

Marco Polo and his brother meet with Kublai Khan. Polo served the Chinese leader for seventeen years and traveled throughout much of Asia.

In 1298 Marco Polo became a prisoner of Genoa during a war with Venice. There he met a fellow prisoner, Rustichello, who was a romance writer. According to Daniel Boorstin, "Marco Polo must somehow have managed to secure his notes from home. Then, profiting from his enforced leisure and from their confinement together, the Venetian dictated a copious letter about his travels to Rustichello, who wrote it all down." One statement in Marco Polo's *Travels* especially captured the attention of Columbus. Marco had said that on the far eastern side of the Great Khan's Asian empire, the islands of Cipango (Japan) were 1,500 miles off the Chinese coast. For this to be true, it seemed that Asia had to practically wrap around the earth toward Europe by means of these islands. In addition, Marco had written: "The noble island of Cipango is a rich source of gold, pearls, and precious stones, and they cover the temples and the royal residences with solid gold."

Marco's information also stimulated the ideas of the astronomer Paolo Toscanelli. On June 25, 1474, Toscanelli had written a now-famous letter to Fernâo

A Secret Journey

In this excerpt, Bartolomé de Las Casas, in his History of the Indies, *discusses the importance of secrecy regarding navigation routes to new overseas territories and the potential wealth they might contain.*

"The King of Portugal wormed more and more information out of Christopher Columbus and . . . secretly equipped a caravel . . . to follow the route Columbus had charted out for himself. . . . [Since] this was a time of feverish activities to and from Guinea, the Azores, Madeira, and Puerto Santo Islands, pretexts were not hard to find to explain the departure of a caravel. . . . When the caravel had sailed many leagues out to sea without finding anything, a fierce storm forced it back to Lisbon.

When the people of Lisbon saw the caravel in such bad shape, they asked where it came from. At first the sailors only muttered things, but soon they were spelling out the reason so that, when Columbus heard it, he knew he had been the object of a double deal and he decided to leave Portugal and come to Castile.

In the charts made in times past, there were depicted certain islands in that sea and vicinity, especially the island of Antilla, and they placed it little more than 200 leagues west of the Canaries and the Azores. . . . The Portuguese still believe it may be the island of the Seven Cities which many have searched for and failed."

Martins to be shown to King Alfonso of Portugal. The letter was accompanied by a nautical map of the Atlantic based on Marco Polo's information. When Columbus received a copy of this letter and map from Toscanelli in 1481, he was more convinced than ever that he could cross the Atlantic. The letter stated:

I was glad to hear of your intimacy and friendship with your most serene and magnificent King. I have often before spoken of a sea route from here to the Indies, where the spices grow, a route shorter than the one which you are pursuing by way of Guinea. You tell me that His Highness desires from me some statement or demonstration that would make it easier to understand and take that route. I should do this by using a sphere shaped like the earth, but I decided that it would be easier and make the point clearer if I showed that route by means of a sea-chart. I therefore send His Majesty a chart drawn by my own hand, upon which is laid out the western coast from Ireland on the north to the end of Guinea, and the islands which lie on that route, in front of which, directly to the west, is shown the beginning of the Indies, with the islands and places at which you are bound to arrive... before you reach those places most fertile in all sorts of spices, jewels, and precious stones. And do not marvel at my calling "west" the regions where the spices grow, although they are commonly called "east"; because whoever sails westward will always find those lands in the west, while one who goes overland to the east will always find the same lands in the east.... And that you may be well informed about all those regions, ... you must know that none but merchants live and trade in all those islands. There is as great a number of ships and mariners with their

Other New World Voyages

Fernando's biography says Columbus was aware of earlier navigators who had ventured forth into the Atlantic. The Norsemen made a landing in north America about five hundred years before Columbus's voyages. None of these journeys had any lasting impact on Europe or the Americas.

"In 1484 an inhabitant of ... Madeira came to Portugal to ask the King for a caravel in order to discover some land which he swore he saw ... [to the west]; his story agreed with that of others who claimed to have seen it from an island of the Azores. On the basis of such stories, the ... maps of ancient days showed certain islands in that region. Aristotle in his book *On Marvelous Things* reports a story that some Carthaginian merchants sailed over the Atlantic.... This island some Portuguese showed on their charts under the name of Antillia, ... two hundred leagues due west of the Canaries and the Azores. [They believe] this is the Island of the Seven Cities, settled by the Portuguese [when] the Moors conquered Spain [714 A.D.].... They say that at that time seven bishops embarked from Spain and came with their ships and people to this island, where each founded a city; and in order that their people might give up all thought of returning to Spain they burned their ships.... They say that in the time of [Henry the Navigator] there arrived at ... Antillia a Portuguese ship, driven there by a storm.... On that island, the ship's boys gathered sand for the firebox and found that it was one third fine gold."

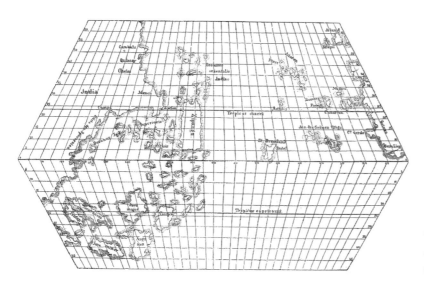

Toscanelli's map proved to Columbus that he could sail west to reach the Far East.

merchandise here as in all the rest of the world, especially in a very noble port called Zaiton [in China], where every year they load and unload a hundred large ships laden with pepper, besides many other ships loaded with other spices. This country is very populous, with a multitude of provinces and kingdoms and cities without number, under the rule of a prince who is called the Great Khan, which name in our speech signifies King of Kings, who resides most of the time in the province of Cathay. . . . This country is as rich as any that has ever been found; not only could it yield great gain and many costly things, but from it may also be had gold and silver and precious stones and all sorts of spices in great quantity, which at present are not carried to our countries. And it is true that many learned men, philosophers and astronomers, and many other men skilled in all the arts, govern this great province and conduct its wars. From the city of Lisbon due west there are twenty-six spaces marked on the map,

each of which contains two hundred and fifty miles, as far as the very great and noble city of Quinsay [in China]. This city is about one hundred miles in circumference, which is equal to thirty-five leagues, and has ten marble bridges. Marvelous things are told about its great buildings, its arts, and its revenues. That city lies in the province of Mangi, near the province of Cathay, in which the king resides the greater part of the time. And from the island of Antillia, which you call the Island of the Seven Cities, to the very noble island of Cipango, there are ten spaces, which make 2,500 miles, that is eight hundred and twenty-five leagues. This land is most rich in gold, pearls, and precious stones, and the temples and royal palaces are covered with solid gold. But because the way is not known, all these things are hidden and covered, though one can travel thither with all security. . . . I remain ready to serve His Highness and answer his questions at greater length if he should order me to do so.[5]

Ancient Measurements

In 200 B.C. the Greeks knew the earth was round, for Eratosthenes measured the circumference of the earth. Carl Sagan's book Cosmos *shows how he did it.*

"[Eratosthenes] was also the director of the great library of Alexandria [Egypt], where one day he read in a papyrus book that in the southern frontier outpost of Syene . . . at noon on June 21 [the temple columns] cast no shadows. . . . A reflection of the Sun could then be seen in the water at the bottom of a deep well. The Sun was directly overhead. . . .

How could it be that at the same instant there was no shadow at Syene and a substantial shadow at Alexandria? The only possible answer, he saw, was that the surface of the Earth is curved."

Eratosthenes used the shadows he saw to determine the circumference of the earth. He drew an imaginary line from the edge (or top) of the shadow in Alexandria to the top of the column. This line formed angle A of seven degrees from the column. Next he measured the distance between the two cities. It was about 5,050 stades (800 kilometers or 500 miles). If the columns in each city are imagined as extending to the center of the earth, they would meet at the same seven-degree angle B (since opposite interior angles are equal). This angle also equals seven degrees on the arc of the earth between the two cities. If, then, 5,050 stades or 500 miles is seven degrees of the earth's surface (of 360 degrees), it is also 7/360th (about 1/50th) of the earth's circumference. And this must be 252,500 stades or 24,750 miles (approximately 50 x 500).

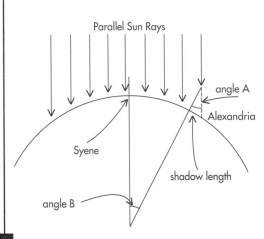

Parallel Sun Rays

angle A

Alexandria

Syene

shadow length

angle B

According to Columbus's contemporary, Bartolemé de Las Casas, Toscanelli's "map set Columbus's mind ablaze." It showed that a westward Atlantic voyage might indeed be successful in reaching the lands of the khan. Marco Polo's islands, with their "temples and royal residences covered with solid gold," would be "stepping stones" along the way.

Another book that influenced Columbus and others in his time was *The Voyage and Ordeal of Sir John Mandeville: A Description of the Way to Jerusalem and the Marvels of the Indies and Other Lands and Countries.*

This book made its appearance about 1370. John Noble Wilford, author of a biography of Columbus, described the book as follows:

> Writing in French in the middle of the fourteenth century, this unknown writer—Mandeville is a *nom de plume* —borrowed from ancient and medieval accounts in telling of travels to the marvelous East, where there were

A drawing from The Voyage and Ordeal of Sir John Mandeville: A Description of the Way to Jerusalem and the Marvels of the Indies and Other Lands and Countries. *This book contained many fantastic, inaccurate tales that Columbus fully accepted as true.*

men with no heads but eyes on their shoulders, men with heads of dogs and feet of horses, and men with ears so long the flaps covered their entire bodies, making clothing unnecessary . . . men with tails . . . islands inhabited only by women.[6]

People in Europe had no way of disproving these statements. To many they might well have been statements of actual fact, especially when they were intermingled with more believable ideas. From many of Columbus's writings it is evident that he was familiar with this book.

The Age of Overseas Navigation Begins

These intellectual discoveries were only one factor in making Columbus's voyage possible. Columbus would not have made his journey without the advances in ship technology that had also taken place. The types of ships capable of making the transatlantic journey were developed in the early fifteenth century. Caravels and carracks had deep holds for cargo and ballast and were equipped with stern-hung rudders. With three masts on each ship that carried both square sails for speed and triangular sails for maneuverability, they could sail anywhere and in any winds. The ships also carried cannons to aid in defense of precious cargoes. The ships would take Columbus to the Americas, and the guns would enable the Europeans to conquer.

Other technological advances aided Columbus. Navigation by compass, quadrant, and astrolabe became common in the 1450s. Mariners used these in combination

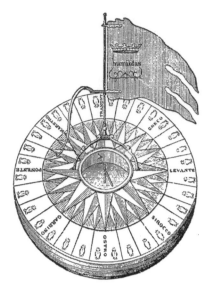

Navigation by compass became common during the 1450s, and Columbus used this technology to make his voyages.

with known heavenly bodies, especially the North Star, which they thought always indicated true north. Even in overcast conditions, the compass pointed directly north, enabling ships to keep to their course. The quadrant and astrolabe were used to keep a ship on its desired north-south latitude. Although their accuracy was limited by choppy waves, these instruments were essential to Columbus's enterprise.

Christopher Columbus's voyage was influenced by the culmination of many reawakened ideas and technological advancements. As he sailed from Palos, Spain, on the first of his momentous voyages on that third day of August 1492, he expected to prove true all of his ideas. Instead, he would make history for very different reasons than he anticipated.

3 The First Voyage

In August 1492, Columbus set out on his first voyage. Propelled by brisk northeasterly winds, his small convoy headed to the southwest toward the Canary Islands; from there they would steer due west for Cipango.

The Voyage

Columbus commanded the flagship, the *Santa Maria*. Martin Alonso Pinzón was the skipper of the *Pinta*. His brother Vincente Yañez Pinzón captained the *Niña*. All three crews were composed of men from Palos, friends of the Pinzóns.

Just four days out, on Grand Canary Island, the crew repaired the *Pinta*'s rudder, which had sprung out of its socket, and they equipped the *Niña* with square rigging. (Square sails were used for speed once the winds were strong.) The whole operation took nearly a month. On September 6, 1492, the small fleet departed the Canaries with square sails billowing and left the known world behind.

Fernando Columbus's biography of his father relates events of Sunday, September 9:

On this day they completely lost sight of land, and many sighed and wept for

Martin Alonso Pinzón accompanied Columbus on his first voyage, and served as the captain of the Pinta.

fear they would not see it again for a long time. The Admiral [Columbus] comforted them with great promises of lands and riches. He decided to

Columbus was skilled in the use of a quadrant, and he used the device to keep his ships on the correct course as he crossed the Atlantic.

below the degrees, or angle of elevation, of the North Star above the horizon. By keeping this angle constant, a ship could keep to the same latitude while sailing east and west. This was especially important for recording a ship's route and for recording where a ship was when it arrived somewhere. In addition, by holding to the same latitude, one could be certain of a correct homeward bearing.

Longitude was a different matter. Columbus did not have a heavenly guide such as the North Star. For north to south sailing, dead reckoning by intuition was the main skill required. The captain of a ship had to estimate his speed and distance traveled by each turn of an hourglass. For this purpose a rope knotted at regular intervals was let out behind the ship for a short period of time. By counting the knots, the captain could calculate the knots-per-hour. A captain's experience at sea was essential to develop a good sense of distance, speed, and time.

Columbus was such a master of this skill that his crew thought he was divinely inspired. Michele de Cuneo, Columbus's friend and shipmate on the second voyage, put it in words: "By a simple look at the night sky, he would know what route to follow or what weather to expect."[8]

As Columbus's voyage continued, certain events caused both admiral and crew to become apprehensive and confused. Some green vegetation and land birds, the first signs of land, appeared as early as on September 16. They were false signs.

The crew's anxiety over these eerie signs was aggravated when something appeared to be wrong with the compass. Columbus's log reads: "The pilots took the north and found that the compass needles varied to the northwest. . . . Every night

understate the number of leagues actually traveled, telling them they had covered only fifteen leagues, though they had actually gone eighteen. He did this that the crew would not think they were so far from Spain as in fact they were, but for himself he kept a secret accurate reckoning.[7]

Columbus knew well the use of the quadrant, which helped keep his ships on the correct latitude. The quadrant was in the shape of a quarter-circle, like a pie slice, marked off from one to ninety degrees. Holding the quadrant with the curved portion below, the sailor sighted the North Star through two pinholes along one straight edge of the quadrant. A weighted thread recorded on the curve the needles moved a whole point away, while at dawn they pointed directly to the Pole Star [North Star]." Columbus figured out what was wrong with their compass: "It appears that the Pole Star describes a circle about the Pole, and the compasses always point true north." They had thought the star was fixed and immobile. Columbus's men were the first Europeans to reach a point on the earth's surface where they could note the normal daily rotation of the North Star.

Besides these concerns, the strong winds that pushed them along worried the men: with such constant easterly winds, how would they get home? Columbus wrote how relieved they all were on September 22, when a contrary westerly

Columbus refused to follow the land birds that were sighted on October 3, 1492. This decision angered his crew and nearly started a mutiny.

One of Columbus's great gifts as a sailor was his ability to accurately gauge his longitudinal position almost by instinct, because no instruments existed to measure it.

wind rose up. That was the wind that would help them get back home.

On October 3, with only the never-ending sea in sight, Martin Alonso Pinzón urged Columbus to detour from course to follow the land birds seen overhead. At first Columbus refused and ordered the fleet to continue on towards Cipango to keep his contract with the Spanish crown. This nearly started a mutiny. Fernando's biography described the details of this near mutiny:

The men met together in the holds of the ships, saying that the Admiral in

Columbus Lands

Based on Columbus's log, Fernando's biography of Columbus describes the first sighting of land in the New World, the first encounter of new peoples, and how his father claimed the land for the king and queen of Spain.

"About two hours after midnight the *Pinta* . . . fired the signal for land. A sailor named Rodrigo de Triana first sighted it. . . . It was not he who received the grant of 10,000 maravedis from the Catholic Sovereigns, however, but the Admiral, who had first seen the light amid the darkness. . . . At daybreak they saw an island about fifteen leagues [40 to 50 miles] in length, very level, full of green trees and abounding in springs, with a large lake in the middle, and inhabited by a multitude of people who hastened to the shore, astounded and marveling at the sight of ships, which they took for animals. . . . The Admiral went ashore with an armed boat, displaying the royal standard. . . . After all had rendered thanks to Our Lord, kneeling on the ground and kissing it, . . . the Admiral arose and gave this island the name San Salvador. Then . . . he took possession of it in the name of the Catholic Sovereigns with appropriate ceremony and words. . . . Many Indians assembled to watch this celebration and rejoicing, and the Admiral, perceiving they were a gentle, peaceful, and very simple people, gave them little red caps and glass beads which they hung about their necks, together with other trifles that they cherished as if they were precious stones of great price."

Columbus and his crew land in the New World.

In this traditional depiction, Columbus plants the Spanish flag on the soil of the New World to claim his "discovery" for Spain.

his mad fantasy proposed to make himself a lord at the cost of their lives or die in the attempt; that they had already tempted fortune as much as their duty required and had sailed farther from land than any others had done. Why, then, should they work their own ruin by continuing that voyage, since they were already running short of provisions and the ships had so many leaks and faults that even now they were not fit to retrace the great distance they had traveled. . . . And since the Admiral's views had been rejected and criticized by many wise and learned men, none would speak in his defense and all would believe what they said. . . . Others said they had heard enough of his gab. If the Admiral would not turn back, they should heave him overboard and report in Spain that he had fallen in accidentally while observing the stars.[9]

The next day Columbus reversed his decision and took Pinzón's advice to steer toward where they would hit the nearest land.

Columbus in the Americas: The First Encounter

On October 11 signals came from the *Pinta* that land was sighted. It was a false alarm. At 10:00 P.M. Columbus spied a light on the horizon, and the helmsman also saw it. Then at 2:00 A.M. on the twelfth, Rodrigo de Triana of the *Pinta* called out: "Tierra!" ("Land!"). The king had promised a reward of 10,000 *maravedis* (coins) to the man who first saw land. But Triana never received his reward. Columbus himself claimed and received the reward.

The land was an island called Guanahaní by its natives. Columbus renamed it San Salvador, in honor of the Christian

Impressions of the Natives

Columbus describes the physical appearance and the peacefulness of the native Americans in his log. This excerpt comes from Fernando's biography of Columbus.

"The Indians followed Columbus even to the ships, some swimming and others paddling in their canoes; they brought parrots, skeins of woven cotton, darts, and other things, which they exchanged for glass beads, hawk's bells, and other trifles. Being a people of primitive simplicity, they all went about as naked as their mothers bore them. . . . Their hair was straight, thick, very black, and short—that is, cut above the ears—though some let it grow down to their shoulders and tied it . . . so that it looked like a woman's tress. They had handsome features, spoiled somewhat by their unpleasantly broad foreheads. They were of middle stature, well formed and sturdy, with olive-colored skins that gave them the appearance of Canary Islanders or sunburned peasants. They had no weapons like ours, nor knew of them: for when the Christians showed them a naked sword, they foolishly grasped it by the blade and cut themselves. . . . Their darts are sticks with sharpened points that they harden in the fire, arming the end with a fish's tooth. . . . They appeared fluent in speech and intelligent, easily repeating words that they had once heard. . . . Many . . . paddled to the ships in their little boats, called canoes; these are made from the trunk of a tree hollowed out . . . all in one piece."

In this painting of Columbus meeting the native Americans, the artist has presented the natives as primitive and subservient, a common European opinion at the time.

holy savior, and "took possession of the said island for the King and for the Queen his Lords." That day the admiral, along with Martin Alonso and Vincente Yañez, were the first men of the Old World of Europe to set foot in the Americas. That small step began a process of encounter and exchange that created the New World.

Soon the Spaniards met their first native Americans. Columbus wrote in his log on the first day in America, Friday, October 12:

> In order that they might be friendly towards us, because I knew that they could more easily be converted to our Holy Faith by love than by force, I gave to some of them red caps, and glass beads . . . and many other things of small value, in which they took so much pleasure and became so much our friends that it was a marvel to see.

The native Americans had absolutely no knowledge of any lands or peoples beyond their immediate island group. The clothed, bearded, and armored Spaniards must have appeared extremely strange to them. The natives had never seen ships as immense as the caravels from Europe.

Columbus's men said the Taínos kissed their feet and treated them as if they were gods. If this is true, it may explain why the Taínos were so friendly, as noted by Columbus in his log. The discovery by the Taínos that the Spaniards were merely humans, and cruel ones at that, would explain their later opposition to Columbus's men.

Columbus's attitude toward the Taínos wavered between admiration and domination. He also believed the islands he encountered and everything on them was his for the taking, including the people. He ends this day's log entry:

> They should be good servants and intelligent, for I observed that they quickly took in what was said to them, and I believe they would easily be made Christians, as it appeared to me that they had no religion. Our Lord pleasing, I will carry off six of them at my departure to Your Highnesses, in order that they may learn to speak.

The idea of ownership was again implicit on October 14, as Columbus wrote:

> We understood that they asked us if we had come from heaven. . . . They are very simple in the use of arms, as Your

Columbus gives European novelties to the native Americans after landing in their homeland.

Highnesses will see from the seven I ordered to be taken back to Castille to learn our language and return, unless Your Highnesses should order them all to be brought to Castille, or to be kept as captives on the same island; for with fifty men I can subjugate them all and make them do whatever we wish.

In keeping with his mission to bring something of value back to the king and queen, Columbus quickly got to the business at hand. On October 13 Columbus asked about the gold . . . and decided to go the next day in search of gold and precious stones. . . . The whole land is so green that it is a pleasure to look on it.

And two days later:

These islands . . . may contain many things of which I have no knowledge, for I do not wish to stop to visit, and so lose time in my search for gold. . . . With the help of our Lord, I will find the origin of this gold.

An Infinite Variety of Food

The first encounters between Europeans and natives were entirely peaceful and trusting. In this selection, Fernando describes some aspects of their culture. He derived this information directly from the log of Columbus's first voyage.

"On November 5th . . . the two Christians [sent out by Columbus to explore] . . . returned. They said they had gone twelve leagues into the interior and had reached a village of fifty large wooden huts, thatched with palms, and shaped like tents or pavilions. . . . The people of the same family live in a single house. . . . All the Indians sat down around them and then came up one by one to kiss their hands and feet, believing they came from Heaven. The Indians also gave them some cooked roots that had the flavor of chestnuts. . . . They met many people who carried a firebrand to light certain herbs the smoke of which they inhale, and to . . . roast those roots of which they had given the Christians to eat and which are their principal food [potatoes]. The Christians also saw an infinite variety of trees, plants . . . and of birds . . . [and] much land planted with the roots mentioned above, . . . beans, . . . and maize [corn, which] is most tasty, boiled, roasted, or ground into flour. . . . Our men saw much cotton. They make no use of it for clothing, but use it rather to make their nets and beds, which they call hammocks."

When Christopher Columbus landed in America, he saw that the natives had small amounts of gold. He began to search for the source of the riches.

Columbus in Cuba

The admiral did indeed hoist sail and leave for a nearby island on October 21. The natives called it Colba (Cuba) and indicated it was a great island; Columbus thought it must be Cipango—the great island of Japan. On October 28 Columbus landed in Cuba and renamed it Juana. At the sight of his caravels, the Cuban natives fled from their village, allowing Columbus and his men an opportunity to explore the village at leisure. The admiral noted in his journal the natives' clean and spacious houses. He thought it was surely a part of some king's lands, and so he ordered the men not to touch anything. Here, surely, he thought, was the source of the gold the natives wore on their noses and ears.

Impressed at Cuba's great size, he wrote on November 1: "It is certain that this is the mainland [of Asia] . . . and I am within a hundred leagues of Quinsay." This city's name was marked several times in the margins of Columbus's copy of Marco Polo's book. Toscanelli's letter had placed it in the province of Mangi in southern China. The next day Columbus sent Luis de Torres, who knew Hebrew, Chaldean, and Arabic, to bring the letters of the Spanish monarchs to the nearest king.

The admiral did not find the Great Khan or the grand cities of Cathay or

Quinsay in Cuba. He found no gold mine either. In his log, he mentions that he found nearly a thousand kinds of fruit and potential profits from trees, mastic, cotton, and aloe. He noted possible settlement sites, always featuring a high hill for a fortress. He also reminded the monarchs that the spread of Christianity had been a primary objective of his sailing:

> Your Highnesses ought not to allow any stranger to trade here or put his foot in the country except Catholic Christians, for this was the beginning and end of the undertaking: namely, the increase and glory of the Christian religion. . . .[10]

On November 18 Martin Alonso Pinzón sailed off in his swift ship, the *Pinta*. Columbus believed Pinzón had convinced the natives to lead him to gold.

Columbus in Hispaniola

The admiral left Cuba on December 9 for a large and beautiful island, known to the local people as Bohio. He called it Hispaniola, or Española, "the Spanish Island" (later known as Santo Domingo island, today Haiti and the Dominican Republic). On the twelfth a woman was taken aboard, and Columbus set a good example for his men of kind treatment of the natives:

> The Admiral caused her to be dressed, and gave her glass beads, hawks' bells, and brass ornaments; then he sent her back to shore very courteously, according to his custom.

On the sixteenth:

> The Admiral ordered them all to be well treated; and he says: 'they are the best people in the world, and the gentlest.'

Pinzón's Betrayal

Once in the New World, Martin Alonso Pinzón went off on his own to find gold. E. G. Bourne, in The Northmen, Columbus, and Cabot, 985–1503, *provides the log entry of January 8, 1493, from Bartolomé de Las Casas's that describes the incident:*

"The Pinzóns had followers filled with pride and avarice, [they considered] that all now belonged to them. And unmindful of the honor the Admiral had done them, they did not obey his orders, but did and said many unworthy things against him; while Martin Alonso had deserted him from the 21st of November [1492] until the 6th of January [1493] without cause or reason. . . . All these things had been endured in silence by the Admiral in order to secure a good end to the voyage. He determined to return as quickly as possible, . . . for it was not a fitting time for dealing out punishment."

I Am Sure I Could Conquer the Entire Island

Columbus's conflicting attitudes toward natives can be seen in the following quote from his log entry of December 26, 1492, taken from E. G. Bourne, The Northmen, Columbus, and Cabot, 985–1503. *It is obvious that he wished the natives to be intimidated by the power of the Spaniards.*

"I assure You that many of my people have asked me to allow them to remain here [in La Navidad]. I have now given orders for a fortress and a tower to be built, . . . and a large moat, not that I believe it be necessary as far as these people are concerned, for, with the men I have on the ships I am sure I could conquer the entire island, which I believe to be larger than Portugal and with more than twice its population. But they go naked and have no weapons and are incorrigible cowards. It is nevertheless proper that this tower should be built, since . . . [the natives] will see the skill and abilities of your Highnesses' subjects, and therefore serve them with love and fear. And they have timber to build the entire fortress, and supplies of bread and wine for more than a year, and seed for sowing, and the ship's boat, and a caulker, a carpenter, a gunner and a cooper. And many of the natives are very anxious to serve Your Highnesses, and to give me the pleasure of finding the mine where the gold is obtained."

In these activities Columbus's gentler side is evident. In the same day's entry he again, however, revealed his intent to conquer the new lands in the name of the king and queen of Spain:

These lands are so good and fertile . . . that no one can adequately describe them and no one could believe if he had not seen them. . . . The only thing lacking is a settlement. . . . and I, with the force I have under me, which is not large, could march over all these islands without opposition [and] the people are so timid . . . that they are good for ordering about, to work and sow, and so all that may be necessary, to build towns, and they should be taught to go about clothed and to adopt our customs.

On December 22 Columbus was invited to the village of King Guacanagarí. The islanders called their kings by the title of *kaseke,* from which the Spanish word *cacique* is derived. The invitation came with a gift of a mask with large ears made of beaten gold. Guacanagarí became a great friend to the Europeans. When, on Christmas Day in 1492, the *Santa Maria* ran aground on a sandbank and was damaged beyond repair, Guacanagarí wept. He sent people who unloaded the ship and moved everything to safe places. Columbus wrote:

Irresistible Objects of Exploitation

This excerpt from Felipe Fernandez-Armesto's book Columbus *attempts to sort out the reasons for the apparent opposition between Columbus's words and deeds: his high admiration for the native Taínos and his shoddy treatment of them.*

On October 12, 1492, Columbus "disembarked to examine the island in the morning light. . . . Before noticing anything about the land . . . Columbus recorded Europeans' first sight of the natives, whom he called 'naked people.' This was not just a description, but a classification. A . . . reader would have understood that Columbus was [not] confronting . . . the citizens of a civil society [with] legitimate political institutions of their own. . . . They presented, because of their innocence, a unique opportunity for spreading the gospel; . . . and because of their defenselessness, an irresistible object of exploitation. . . . Many of [Columbus's] observations cut two ways. The natives' ignorance of warfare established their [innocence] but also made them 'easy to conquer.' Their nakedness evoked a [Garden of Eden] . . . but also suggested savagery and similarity to beasts. . . . The way they exchanged treasures for trifles showed that they were both morally uncorrupted and easily duped. Their rational faculties made them [both] identifiable as humans and exploitable as slaves. Columbus's attitude was not necessarily duplicitous, only ambiguous. He was genuinely torn between two conflicting ways of classifying the Indians."

Not a pin was missing. . . . They are a loving people, without covetousness, . . . and I assure Your Highnesses that there is no better land nor people. They love their neighbors as themselves and their speech is the sweetest and gentlest in the world and always with a smile.[11]

On Bohio, Columbus decided to build a colony with a strong fortress and tower, which he called La Navidad, symbolizing the birth of Jesus and of New Spain. As he wrote on December 26: "I recognized that Our Lord had caused the ship to run aground there, in order that I might found a settlement there."

On December 27, natives told Columbus that the *Pinta* was at the other end of the island. Columbus believed that Martin Alonso had been led by natives to the source of the gold, for the admiral made

The Santa Maria *was wrecked on the shore of Hispaniola, but the native Americans helped Columbus salvage the supplies from his ship.*

plans to hurry home to Castile. In fact, far from disciplining Pinzón and his crew when he learned there was no gold, Columbus "bore Pinzón's desertion in silence to give a good end to the voyage."[12]

But all was not friendly between Columbus and Martin Alonso Pinzón. The admiral wrote on January 3 that he did not wish Pinzón, in the faster *Pinta,* to reach home ahead of him. He feared that Martin Alonso would give the sovereigns a distorted version of the voyage. On January 8 Columbus again wrote very harshly against the "mutinous attitude" of the Pinzón brothers and their men.

Columbus Sets Out on His Return to Spain

Columbus left thirty-nine men in La Navidad to complete the fortress and continue the search for sources of gold. Before daylight on January 16, two ships set out on their return voyage to Europe. On February 14, in mid-Atlantic, a storm caused all to fear for their lives. Columbus even sent a report of the voyage overboard, sealed in a sturdy barrel, in case the ships were lost at sea.

Another storm on March 4, when the vessels were nearing Lisbon, forced the ships to limp into port. Port authorities took the admiral into custody, but King John received Columbus pleasantly, curious about his voyage to "the Indies." A week later, on March 11, he sent Columbus on his way, carrying letters to the Spanish rulers. On March 15, 1493, Christopher Columbus returned to the same Palos port that he had left on the third of August of the year before, having been absent 225 days.

The Admiral's Triumphant Reception

The next months, March to September, were the high point of Columbus's life. In April he reported to the royal couple in

On February 14, 1493, a storm threatened Columbus's ships. The explorer sealed a report of his voyage in a barrel and ordered that it be thrown overboard so that the result of his voyage would be known even if he did not survive.

Barcelona. The city was decorated with all the colors of springtime in honor of the hero's return—the fifteenth century's version of a ticker-tape parade. The monarchs rose to their feet when Columbus entered the reception hall. He was given a chair, and he alone among the courtiers was requested to sit in the presence of the rulers of Spain. He related his story and introduced the near-naked native Americans he had brought with him on the journey. Columbus had taught the natives to recite the Ave Maria and how to cross themselves, which they did before the rulers. The rulers led the assemblage in prayers of thanks and those present could hardly hold back their tears of joy.

In those happy days, Columbus was taxied about in the king's carriage, had dinner with the cardinal, and enjoyed all the privileges of El Almirante (Admiral) of Spain. In May the sovereigns gave Columbus a coat of arms, proof of his nobility. In the same month, he received the 10,000

Columbus was welcomed as a hero when he returned to Spain from the New World for the first time.

Columbus's Triumphant Return

Bartolomé de Las Casas relates in his History of the Indies *Columbus's greatest moment: the Barcelona reception in 1493 after his first voyage.*

"The news spread over Castile like fire that a land called the Indies had been discovered. . . . The roads swelled with throngs come to welcome [Columbus] in the towns through which he passed. . . . Columbus hastened to Barcelona, where he arrived in mid-April. The monarchs . . . had organized a solemn and beautiful reception. . . . The streets were crammed with people come to see this eminent person who had found another world, as well as to see the Indians, the parrots, the gold and other novelties. . . . The King and Queen sat . . . on their royal thrones and next to them sat . . . the highest nobility . . . all beaming with happiness and anxious to greet the hero. . . . Columbus reached the royal stand. He looked like a Roman senator: tall and stately, gray-haired, with a modest smile. . . . [The monarchs] stood up before him as before the highest nobleman. Then on bended knee, he kissed their hands; they kissed his hands and asked him to come sit next to them, a mark of honor Their Highnesses showed only to very few. Columbus told them about . . . his tribulations, the discovery, the greatness and abundance of the new land, . . . showing . . . unpolished gold pieces and nuggets of all sizes. . . . But more important, he . . . praised [the Indians] as . . . gentle people ready to receive the Faith, as could be seen from those Indians who were present. The King and Queen heard this with profound attention and . . . sank to their knees in deep gratitude to God."

Christopher Columbus returns to the king and queen of Spain with native Americans and examples of the New World's riches.

In the days after his return from the New World, Columbus was treated like a noble, admired by the important people in Spain.

maravedis that the sovereigns had promised to the man who first sighted land.

Columbus's Plan for Settlement of the Americas

During April, Columbus presented to the rulers his "Memorial on the Settlement and Government" of the islands of the Indies. Scholar Kirkpatrick Sale called it "a remarkable document . . . undeservedly ignored, inasmuch as it was the first statement of the colonial strategies and policies of empire."[13] Writer E. G. Bourne notes that this document, together with another in 1494, entitles Columbus to be considered the "pioneer lawgiver" of the New World.

According to the report, the islands were to be won and settled by 2,000 Spaniards. Most of the report had to do with gold. Only homesteaders would be allowed to search for gold, and only in "gold-hunting season," so they would have time to farm and do other necessary things. The report did not mention the ruler of Cipango or the Great Khan. And it assumed that the natives and their land were the property of Spain. The only provision Columbus made for the natives was that priests should be sent to instruct them.

Columbus's achievement made little impact in Europe beyond Spain and Portugal. Ferdinand and Isabella wanted

The king and queen of Spain gave Columbus this coat of arms as proof of his noble status.

Only six months after he returned to Spain, Columbus began his second voyage to the New World.

Columbus to return to the islands as soon as possible, for the king of Portugal now also claimed them. News arrived that the Portuguese were already equipping a fleet to take possession. In 1493 the issue was brought before the pope in Rome for a decision. On May 3, 1493 the pope announced that every land discovered by the Spanish was theirs as long as it did not already belong to a Christian prince.

In order to protect and explore the islands further, Columbus left for his second voyage only six months after his return to Spain.

Chapter

4 The Second Voyage

The royal couple needed no persuasion to sponsor Columbus's second voyage. They accepted the reports of the admiral and his men about the potential wealth that might be amassed for Spain in the New World. They were excited about the idea of acquiring vast amounts of land on which Spanish colonists could settle. As for the native Americans, the monarchs agreed with and accepted Columbus's plan to convert them to Catholicism. The royal couple provided funds for seventeen caravels and a crew of 1,200 to 1,500 settlers, including about four hundred soldiers who could defend the settlers in case of emergency. Great optimism filled the air on September 25, 1493, the day Columbus departed from Cadiz, a southwestern port in Spain.

Unfortunately, Columbus's exaggerations about the potential gold to be found in the new lands attracted adventurers and opportunists who hoped to get rich quickly and return home. They were not ideal colonists, who would build towns and work the land, but were more like the rough and ready '49ers (gold seekers) who later opened the American West. They would not easily be controlled or governed. Their greed and viciousness would make Columbus's administration of the islands extremely difficult.

Columbus's fleet of ships leaves for his second voyage.

Columbus also took along a variety of animals, including horses, cows, chickens, and pigs, common species that did not yet exist in the Americas. European plants such as wheat, barley, and shoots of sugarcane were brought over as well. With these plants and animals Columbus hoped to establish a New Spain, with farms and ranches dotting the countryside. Descendants of these animals and plants would alter the New World drastically.

Columbus unintentionally brought from Europe other items that would have just as lasting an impact on the New World: the ships' crews and passengers carried several strains of European germs. Diseases such as measles, typhus, tuberculosis, influenza, scarlet fever, and worst of all, smallpox would prove to have a devastating effect on the natives of the New World. The native Americans had no immunity to these diseases and would die by the thousands when exposed to them. This transference of plants, animals, and disease was Columbus's least publicized, but much greater, contribution to the New World than was merely discovering it. These contributions would have a fundamental and lasting impact on native cultures and later settlers.

Native Americans, too, made their own deadly contribution to the Old World. Many of the natives were infected with a deadly strain of the venereal disease syphilis, which they transmitted to the voyagers. When some of these Europeans returned to the Old World in the spring of 1494, they carried the disease with them and infected others. Because the first major outbreak in Europe of this syphilis occurred among French troops fighting Spaniards in Italy that year, it became known as the "French disease."

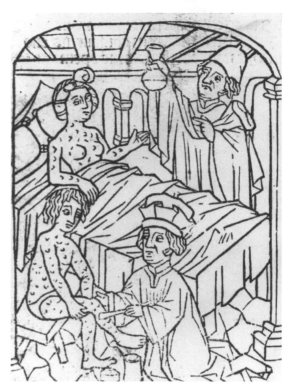

Thousands of native Americans died from smallpox, a disease the Europeans brought to the New World.

First Landfall of Second Voyage

The fleet's first landfall on the way back to the settlement of La Navidad was aptly named Dominica (Sunday Island), since it occurred on Sunday, November 2, 1493. Other islands named by Columbus on this voyage were the Virgin Islands, Puerto Rico, Santo Tomas, and Jamaica—in general, the islands of the Lesser Antilles. In addition to naming these new places, Columbus explored the southern coast of Cuba.

The Reality of a Savage Frontier

Columbus had to report the massacre at La Navidad in a manner that maintained the monarchs' confidence in him. In his book Columbus, *Felipe Fernandez-Armesto analyzes the admiral's state of mind in the face of this disaster.*

"Columbus's own state of mind, . . . emerges from his memorandum . . . to Ferdinand and Isabella . . . at the end of January 1494. It was an attempt to salvage his reputation. . . . It opens with . . . reassurances and praise of Hispaniola's potential: this is Columbus's attempt to bolster royal confidence in his now discredited judgment. A series of damning admissions follow. . . . One by one, Columbus's earlier false predictions—about the gold, the climate, the Indians—are stripped away and the horrible reality of life on a savage frontier is exposed. Columbus interweaves excuses with the admissions; some of the disasters—such as the worst of all, the massacre—are reported only indirectly. . . . Columbus turns quickly to a vision of the island's future, to which he devotes a great deal of space and detail. . . . The islands are to be . . . planted with wheat, vines, and sugar and grazed by Castilian livestock. The natives are to be subjugated and converted to Christianity, wrenched into a European way of life or exported as slaves. . . . [Settlers] will engage in petty industry or commerce or the military occupation of the territory. . . . [Columbus] pleads for men who will have a stake in the long-term success, rather than just . . . exploitation. . . . Finally, Columbus turned to his abiding preoccupation with his own share of the profits."

Columbus and his men held religious services in an attempt to convert the native Americans to Christianity.

Native Americans led by Caonabó burn the settlement of La Navidad and kill its inhabitants.

Trouble in Paradise: La Navidad Is Destroyed, Isabela Is Founded

Cheerfulness and anticipation dissolved to sorrow on November 28, when the fleet finally reached La Navidad. Columbus hoped to see a flourishing colony. Instead, all thirty-nine Spaniards he had left behind were dead, and La Navidad lay in ashes. No gold was found. The tribesmen of Columbus's old friend, the *kaseke* Guacanagarí, arrived at the town and related what had happened. As Fernando describes it,

> They could say some words in Spanish and knew the names of all the Christians who had been left there. Soon after the Admiral's departure those men began to quarrel among themselves, each taking as many women and as much gold as he could. [Eleven of the men] left with their women for the country of the cacique named Caonabó, who was lord of the mines. Caonabó killed them, and some days later marched with a strong force against Navidad, which was held only by Diego de Arana and ten other men who were willing to remain and guard the fortress, all the others having dispersed to various places on the island. Arriving by night, Caonabó set fire to the houses in which the Christians lived with their women, forcing them to flee to the sea, where eight of them drowned; three others . . . were killed ashore. Guacanagarí fought against Caonabó in defense of the Christians, but was wounded and had to flee.[14]

Columbus sent one of his lieutenants, Pedro Margarit, to capture Chief Caonabó to punish him for his crimes against the settlers and to locate Caonabó's gold mines. Margarit was unable to accomplish either of these tasks.

The events at La Navidad shocked Columbus. He began to realize that the native Americans could be provoked to war. He decided to build his next colonial settlement like a fortress, which he located on the northeastern coast of Hispaniola to the east of La Navidad. Columbus called it Isabela, for his queen. The whole project was a failure from the start. Because the Europeans refused to eat America's abundant foods, they began to suffer from malnutrition and could not work. Columbus tried to get the soldiers to pitch in, but

Poor Morale Complicates the Completion of Isabela

Finding La Navidad in ruins, Columbus planned a second, better-fortified settlement, Isabela. Bartolomé de Las Casas relates in his History of the Indies *the immense difficulties Columbus faced in mobilizing the men of his seventeen-ship second voyage to work on the building project.*

"The location [of Isabela] is rich in stones, tiles, and good earth for the making of bricks, besides being fertile and beautiful. [Columbus] hastened to . . . the building of a fort, . . . a church, a hospital and a sturdy house for himself. He distributed land plots, traced a common square and streets. . . . and everyone was told to start building his own house. . . . But the men were exhausted from such a long voyage. . . . In addition, the climate was different, Spanish food was rationed, and because of their newness, the native [foods] produced ill effects . . . and many died. . . . To make things worse, they were sad and frustrated, being so far from home and not having found the gold. . . . The Admiral was sick like everyone else, for his task at sea had been immense and [without adequate] sleep. . . . His was a new route known only to himself; consequently, the responsibility for the whole fleet fell upon his shoulders, a responsibility unlike any other in that he had the whole world in suspense, waiting to see what would come of this enterprise, and he had the obligation to satisfy the King of Castile. . . . Also, the monetary and human investment was greater this time than for the first voyage."

they refused. The soldiers believed that such manual labor was beneath them. Finally, Columbus, too, became sick.

The Quest for Gold Goes On

Gold remained Columbus's chief objective. According to a letter dated January 20, 1494, by his friend and crewman, Michele de Cuneo, gold was "the main reason he had started on so great a voyage full of so many dangers." While continuing to try to build Isabela, Columbus heard the natives of Hispaniola speak of a nearby island called Cibao. His ears heard "Cipango," and he remembered Marco Polo's "golden houses." Work ceased at Isabela and Columbus set out for Cibao. But when he arrived he learned that Cibao meant "rocky land" and had nothing to do with Cipango. Some gold dust found there, however, encouraged him to build a fort there named Santo Tomas.

Cuneo wrote, "Indians brought three big pieces of gold. . . . With this he and all of us made merry, not caring any longer about any sort of spicery but only of this blessed gold."[15] But neither gold mines nor river lodes were ever found.

In February 1494 Columbus sent twelve ships back to Spain. The ships carried twenty-six natives, who were to learn Spanish and become interpreters. Columbus also sent back about 104,000 grams (230 pounds) of gold and sixty parrots. The amount of gold was much less than Columbus had hoped for. The ships carried a letter written by Michele de Cuneo and another by fleet physician Diego Alvarez

This 1494 woodcut shows the settlement of Isabela, a fortressed site Columbus and his men built to replace La Navidad.

Chanca, which both survive today and are major sources for the events of the second voyage.

The returning ships also carried Columbus's extensive report to the king and queen. He again exaggerated the amounts of gold still to be found in the islands and requested that caravels be sent to him with more provisions:

> I sent two men to discover, each in a different direction, and each without remaining long on his mission found so many rivers, so filled with gold, that all those who saw it and collected it, merely with their hands as specimens, . . . say great things about its abundance. . . . I would have sent more . . . if only our people here had not fallen suddenly ill. . . . We especially require wine . . . sheep and lambs . . . raisins, sugar, almonds, honey, and rice . . . goats . . . pigs . . . donkeys . . . seed corn . . . muskets, powder and shot . . . and molasses. . . . Since there is here no interpreter, through whom we might give these people understanding of our holy Faith, . . . there are now sent with these ships some of the [Caníbales, or Caribs], . . . that they be able better to learn our language . . . and become interpreters. . . . Please also send caravels here every year with cattle and other supplies. . . . Payment for these things could be made to the shippers in slaves from among the [Caníbales].

Although no one can say exactly why Columbus exaggerated to the king and queen, it is likely that he feared they would withdraw their support if he told the truth. As it was, the monarchs responded to his request by sending Columbus's brother

In 1494, Columbus took three ships to explore the coast of Cuba. He hoped to prove that it was connected to the continent of Asia.

Bartolomé with three caravels loaded with the requested provisions, which arrived four months later, on June 24, 1494.

Columbus Explores Cuba

From April 24 to September 29, 1494, Columbus took three ships to explore Juana (modern Cuba), leaving his brother Diego in charge at Isabela. Columbus set out to prove that Cuba was an extension of the continent of Asia. Sailing Cuba's south coast, his ships detoured to Jamaica on a ten-day treasure hunt for gold. Although they endured a storm, hostile natives, and damaged ships, they found no gold on Jamaica.

Returning to Cuba, Columbus and his men followed the coast for over 1000 miles. No European had ever heard of an island that large: Columbus thought it must be

Columbus's brother Bartolomé arrived on June 24, 1494, with more provisions for Christopher and the settlers.

Asia, even though there was no evidence that it was. To verify his idea, however, Columbus made his men swear and sign their names to an oath that Cuba was in fact a mainland and that if they had sailed farther, they would have found the Chinese.

Fernando described his father as being quite sick during the exploration of Cuba:

By this time the Admiral was completely exhausted, both because of the poor food and because, apart from the eight days when he had been seriously ill, he had not taken off his clothes or spent a whole night in bed from the time he left Spain to May 19th [1494], when he set this [account of the exploration of Cuba] down in his journal.[16]

Would-Be Settlers Denounce Columbus

The friction among Columbus, his settlers, and the natives became serious during the second period in the New World. Felipe Fernandez-Armesto explains why in this reading from his book Columbus.

"The fault, in a sense, was Columbus's own. The picture he had painted of large quantities of gold for the picking and willing Indians to serve, all in a healthy climate and fertile soil, had been taken literally . . . and had attracted the idlers and fly-by-nights it deserved. . . . [and] provoked disillusionment when the men found how hostile the environment really was and how great the labour demanded of them.

[Columbus wrote] 'None of the settlers came save in the belief that the gold and spices could be gathered in by the shovelful, and they did not reflect that, though there was gold, it would be buried in mines, and the spices would be on the treetops and that the gold would have to be mined and the spices harvested and cured—all of which I made public . . . in Seville, because those who wished to come were so numerous. And I knew what they were after and so I had this explained to them, with all the work that men who go to settle far-away lands for the first time, and they all replied that it was to do such work that they were going.'

It became a not unusual sight for disappointed colonists, returning from Hispaniola, to riot before the monarchs at their public audiences, denouncing Columbus."

The Conquest of Hispaniola

While Columbus was gone, the community at Isabela fell into complete disarray under Diego's leadership. When Columbus returned at the end of September, he found settlers starving, sick, or dead. He, too, still suffered from a fever and drowsiness, loss of sight, and loss of memory. Fernando wrote,

> The Spaniards [Margarit's men, returned from their failed mission] at Isabela went among the Indians, stealing their property and wives and inflicting so many injuries upon them that the Indians resolved to avenge themselves.[17]

Columbus ordered those Spaniards who had mistreated the natives to be flogged or to have their ears and noses slit. Columbus's men felt this was extremely harsh treatment and many of them began to hate and turn against him. Columbus also punished the native tribesmen who had killed Christians. Although the natives had merely defended themselves, Colum-

---

Margarit Sows Seeds of Discord

This selection from Fernando's biography reflects Columbus's conviction, when he returned from his exploration of Cuba, that the people around him were the causes of the breakdown of his administration. As was his custom, Columbus's punishment consisted of enslaving, not killing, the natives.

[Columbus] "found that most of the Indians of the country had risen in revolt through the fault of Pedro Margarit. . . . At the time of his departure for Cuba the Admiral had appointed this man captain over 360 foot soldiers . . . with instructions to patrol the country and reduce it to the service of the Catholic Sovereigns. . . . Instead [Margarit] proved to be the prime cause of the discords and factions that arose in Isabela. . . . In the end, . . . being unwilling to await the arrival of the Admiral, to whom he would have had to account for his actions in office, [Margarit] embarked on the first ships that came from Castile, without . . . making any disposition of the [360] men left in his charge. As a result each one went . . . among the Indians, stealing their property and wives and inflicting so many injuries upon them that the Indians resolved to avenge themselves. . . . On his return [from Cuba] the Admiral severely punished these actions. . . . [The natives] were seized and sent as prisoners to Castile. . . . Caciques had already slain many Christians and would have killed many more if the Admiral had not stopped them in time."

---

bus knew he must not allow them to believe they could harm Christians. Columbus was learning about the loneliness of leadership.

To make matters worse, Columbus learned that in his absence Margarit and other disappointed settlers had seized Bartolomé's caravels and sailed for home. Columbus knew that once back in Spain, they would complain to the monarchs that there really was no gold and that the natives were not all that friendly. They would accuse the admiral of misleading the king and queen and the settlers about the attractions of the New World.

In the midst of these troubles, news arrived that Chief Caonabó was preparing to attack the Christians because of their continued atrocities against his people. The walls of Isabela had not yet been completed, and the situation had become dangerous. Columbus responded by sending a punitive expedition against the natives, both Caribs and Taínos, who had dared attack the Christians. This mission returned to Isabela with sixteen hundred native prisoners. The danger was temporarily over.

Spain's Treaty of Tordesillas with Portugal

In November 1494, Antonio de Torres arrived with four resupply ships. He also carried a letter from Queen Isabella. The letter was addressed to "My Admiral." It announced the June 1494 Treaty of Tordesillas with Portugal: a north-south line was selected, about 1,500 miles (370 leagues) west of the Cape Verde Islands. The treaty allotted to Spain the portion of the Atlantic Ocean and all lands west of the line, and to Portugal all lands in the eastern Atlantic, to recognize Portugal's explorations

of the west African coast. Brazil lay in the Portuguese side. This treaty was accepted throughout Europe because of the immense authority of the pope, who also signed it. The queen asked Columbus to determine where this line was in the Atlantic. She requested maps and other news from the islands. Because of what she had heard from Margarit about the treatment of the natives, Isabella strongly forbade the taking of slaves.

The admiral had little good news and little gold to send her in return. Despite the queen's command regarding the taking of slaves, Columbus thought he could please Isabella by sending an extremely large number of slaves. When Torres returned to Castile on February 24, 1495, his four caravels bulged with five hundred slaves. The admiral's son Diego and his friend Michele de Cuneo also returned to Spain at this time. Cuneo wrote that two

This map shows the division of territory under the 1494 Treaty of Tordesillas. Portugal controlled land east of the line, and Spain controlled land west of the line.

The Whole Affair Is a Joke

Las Casas relates in his History of the Indies *how Margarit and other returning colonists tried to discredit Columbus's enterprise. Despite his setbacks, Columbus still had a good-enough reputation to merit the financing of a third voyage.*

"Pedro Margarit and other noblemen . . . informed the King that he should not entertain any hopes of acquiring wealth in the Indies, for the whole affair was a joke, there simply was no gold on the island. . . . The King began to conceive of Columbus's enterprise as a waste of money, which was reinforced by the fact that these gentlemen had not brought any gold with them. [He should have realized] that gold does not grow on trees but in mines under the ground and that nowhere in the world has gold ever been extracted without toil unless it be stolen from someone else's chests. Columbus had brought ample proof of the . . . gold both when he returned from his first voyage and when he dispatched Antonio de Torres back to Castile with the gold his men had extracted and the gold given him by Guacanagarí. . . . The King [sent] . . . Juan Aguado, to spy on [Columbus]. . . . In October 1495, when the Admiral was engaged in the war against King Caonabó. . . . Indian chiefs . . . discussed the benefits that might result from a new admiral since the old one so mistreated them; but they were mistaken, for every Spaniard who ever went to the Indies added new injuries to the old ones and drove them infernally until they were extinguished. . . . Little attention was paid to [Aguado's report]."

hundred natives died at sea not far from Spain. The rest were returned later to America.

In June 1495 Columbus's general Alonso de Hojeda, who had been sent out to meet peacefully with native *kasekes*, tricked Caonabó into putting on bright silver cuffs and leg-irons as the proper attire for peace talks. Caonabó's capture set off more native uprisings, but finally peace was again restored. Nevertheless, relations between native Americans and Europeans would never be the same again.

The Tribute and the *Encomienda* System

Columbus now badly needed to return to Spain to answer the complaints of Margarit's men by producing real gold. In

Native Americans pan for gold in island streams. Columbus demanded that the native Americans bring him gold to send back to Spain.

the plan assigned several natives to each colonist to help them build and farm. Since slavery was prohibited by law, however, the natives were supposed to be repaid for their services by being instructed in the Christian faith. But the instruction almost never took place.

In October 1495, while Columbus was preparing for his return to Spain, the king and queen sent over a team led by Juan Aguado to investigate Columbus's supervision of the colonies. Aguado was pleased with Columbus's governorship, including the *encomienda* system. Unfortunately, after Columbus left, the *encomienda* became essentially a slave system.

order to save face, he came up with a plan to obtain the gold that he was sure the natives knew of but refused to deliver. In 1495 he demanded that all Taínos over the age of fourteen had to bring him a hawk's bell (the size of a thimble) full of gold or twenty-five pounds of spun cotton every three months. Failure to do so led to punishment, which, some witnesses maintained, meant having their hands cut off. At first the natives easily met their quota by contributing the small bits of gold they had accumulated through the years. When this was used up, the natives had great difficulty producing the required quota of gold. In this way Columbus accumulated some gold and cotton with which he hoped to impress Ferdinand and Isabella.

Hoping to prevent another disaster between the natives and the colonists, Columbus set up a labor system before he returned to Spain. Called the *encomienda,*

Columbus Returns from His Second Voyage

Columbus headed back to Spain, arriving in March 1496. He and his crew traveled on the *Niña* and one other vessel. Although each of the caravels had a normal capacity of about 25 passengers, on this voyage they carried 225 Spaniards and 30 natives, including Caonabó, who still wore the silver chains. It was a stormy voyage, which Caonabó did not survive.

Upon his return, Columbus was questioned by the Spanish monarchs about his men's accusations of cruelty and misgovernment. The monarchs were aware that since Columbus had arrived, the native American population in the islands had been severely reduced by disease and harsh treatment. In addition, warfare frequently broke out between Christians and natives. The Taínos, who might have been peaceful subjects of Catholic Spain, had become rebels and had still not been converted. The sources of gold had not been found. Although Columbus managed to convince Ferdinand and Isabella that he could improve the situation, they had lost confidence in him.

In addition to answering these charges, Columbus had to face the embarrassing fact that he had not reached Asia. John Cabot discovered North America for the British in 1497, and the Portuguese admiral Vasco da Gama reached the real Indies in 1498. Cabot's accomplishment brought Great Britain into the race for territory and trade; da Gama's voyage meant that Portugal had won her race with Spain to gain independent trade with Asia and the wealth that would surely follow.

Columbus had ample time to think about these developments while he was in Castile. Since he had failed to find gold, spices, or the Indies, he must have wondered precisely where he had been and what he could hope to gain from the place.

Harsh "Justice"

Bartolomé de Las Casas condemned Spanish cruelty toward the natives. Las Casas had praised Columbus's heroic crossing of the Atlantic but was also aware of his human shortcomings, as this quotation from the History of the Indies *attests.*

"Some natives had stolen bundles of Spanish clothes and taken them to their cacique. In retaliation, on Wednesday, April 9, 1494, Alonso de Hojeda took some 400 men inland and . . . came upon a town, chained its cacique, his brother and one of his nephews and sent them as prisoners to the Admiral. Moreover, he caught a relative of the cacique and had his ears cut off in the public square. The cacique of the nearby town, trusting in the welcome he . . . had given both the Admiral and Hojeda on their first visit, decided to . . . plead with the Admiral not to harm his friends. When the prisoners arrived and he with them, the Admiral ordered a crier to announce their public decapitation. What a pretty way to promote justice, friendship, and make the [Christian] Faith appealing—to capture a King in his own territory and sentence him . . . to death, for no fault of [his] own! Even if they were guilty, the crime was so [small] it begged for moderation. . . . When the other cacique . . . heard the sentence, he begged the Admiral to save them and with tears promised as best he could by sign language that nothing of the sort would ever happen again, and the Admiral granted his plea by revoking the sentence."

John Cabot discovers North America for the English. The explorations of Cabot and Vasco da Gama forced Columbus to acknowledge that he had not discovered Asia.

In February 1498 he wrote out his will. In it he named Genoa, Italy, as his homeland, and his sons Diego and Fernando as primary heirs. His brothers and Fernando's mother, Beatríz were also included

Ferdinand and Isabella did not permit Columbus to return to the New World until July 1498. This time Columbus left his brother Bartolomé in command of Isabela, with instructions to found another town. His new town, named Santo Domingo, was constructed on the southern coast of Hispaniola. It was destined to become the oldest continuously inhabited settlement in the Americas.

5 Columbus's Last Voyages

Ferdinand and Isabella gave Columbus very specific orders for his third voyage. Columbus was to attempt to persuade settlers to remain permanently in the New World. As an incentive, settlers would be given land. The monarchs also demanded that Columbus treat the natives fairly, renew attempts to convert them, and forbid slavery. Columbus sailed with six ships laden with provisions. He had a more difficult time finding settlers willing to go with him, however. Columbus's crews were made up of released convicts on condition that they serve aboard his ships. The dismal reports of disappointed colonists about life in the islands had spoiled Columbus's credibility.

While he loaded supplies in the Canaries, Columbus sent three of his ships directly to Santo Domingo. His own flagship and two others followed. Once he arrived in the New World in early August 1498, he did not sail directly to Santo Domingo. Instead, he explored the western Atlantic area. This exploration proved to be very important to the admiral, for this time he really did find a continent. But it was not Asia. Columbus was the first European to set foot in South America (Venezuela), two years before the Portuguese Pedro Cabral

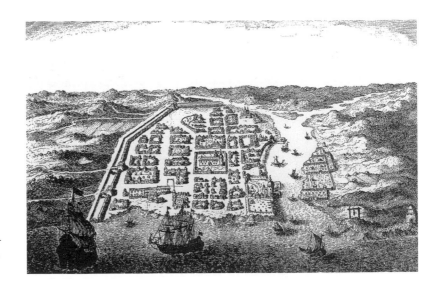

The settlement of Santo Domingo. Columbus sent three supply ships to reprovision the settlers at the beginning of his third voyage.

Columbus's Critics

Columbus was well aware of what his critics were saying about him. E. G. Bourne in The Northmen, Columbus, and Cabot, 985–1503, *quotes several passages of the* Lettera Rarissima *where Columbus defended his reputation. Responding to those who had called him a poor admiral, he said they should know that on such a voyage as this, many unexpected difficulties may arise:*

"My ships were worm-eaten and I still had to traverse 7,000 miles of sea. . . . Those who are accustomed to find fault and to censure, asking from their safe places, 'Why was not so and so done in that case?' let them make answer now. I could have used them on this voyage; I truly believe that another voyage of another kind [to Hell] is in store for them, or our Faith is in vain."

As if in anticipation of modern critics who make him personally the cause of all the inhuman treatment of the native Americans, Columbus wrote:

"Seven years I was at your royal court, where all to whom this enterprise was mentioned unanimously declared it to be a delusion. Now all of them, down to the very tailors, seek permission to make discoveries. . . . They go forth to plunder, and it is granted to them to do so, so that they greatly prejudice my honor and do very great damage to the enterprise."

---

landed in Brazil. He wrote to the rulers on October 18, 1498:

I have come to believe that this is a mighty continent which was hitherto unknown. I am greatly supported in this view because of this great river [Orinoco] and by this sea [Gulf of Paria] which is fresh.[18]

Soon after this, Columbus began to refer to his discoveries as *otro mundo* (another world). This term indicates a growing awareness on his part that he had not reached the Asian Indies at all.

If this land mass was not Asia, but some other continent—another world—then Columbus must also have suspected that all his claims about reaching Cipango's offshore islands and about Cuba's being part of Asia had been wrong. Columbus began to argue that this new land mass whose existence nobody could have predicted was the actual Garden of Eden or, as he called it, the "Terrestrial Paradise." This spectacular discovery would be much more important than finding even the khan or the gold. Once this news reached Europe, he thought, his lost reputation would be restored.

In his insistence that he had discovered Eden, Columbus revealed his lack of education. For many years Columbus had been collecting passages from the Bible and elsewhere that he believed confirmed that he had been chosen by God to bring Christianity to the world's heathens. This collection still exists in Columbus's own handwriting and is known as *The Book of Prophecies*. Many of the entries refer to the Terrestrial Paradise as being in or near Asia. Columbus's own confusion about whether he was in a previously uncharted region of Asia or in a land "hitherto unknown" leaves historians questioning just what he did believe at this time.

When Columbus wrote his summary letter of the third voyage to the rulers in October 1498, the incredible discovery of the biblical Terrestrial Paradise filled every page. Columbus's account emphasizes his strongly religious orientation. He remarks that all the signs seemed to say he had

Conversion by Terror

This passage from Las Casas's History of the Indies *places the blame for the poor relationship between the natives and the settlers squarely on Columbus.*

"After all, the Admiral had come without permission, and Christians were such a fierce-looking novelty, trespassing with arms and horses that seemed so ferocious that the mere sight of them made the inhabitants tremble. . . . This was an offense which everyone in the world today [the fifteenth century] would take as such and seek revenge. . . . The worst . . . crime was to capture a King living peacefully in his own domain and to chain him. . . . Reason itself says it was not right to trespass, not right to do it in a warlike manner, and not right that the Admiral leave the ship without first . . . asking permission to do so and sending gifts, as he had been instructed to do by the King of Castile. The Admiral should have taken pains to bring love and peace and to avoid scandalous incidents. . . . Truly, I would not dare blame the Admiral's intentions, for I knew him well and I know his intentions were good. . . . There is much to ponder here and one can see . . . that the Admiral and . . . those who followed after him in this land, worked on the assumption that the way to achieve their desires was . . . to instill fear in these people, . . . making the name Christian synonymous with terror. . . . And this is contrary . . . to the way that those who profess Christian gentleness and peace ought to negotiate the conversion of infidels."

Native Americans and Spanish settlers battle on the island of Hispaniola.

reached a special place. First, the natives were again friendly; they were fairer skinned than on the islands and actually wore clothing. The sea was smoother and the water fresh. Columbus had also come to believe that the earth "has the shape of a pear." He concluded that "I am completely persuaded in my own mind that the Terrestrial Paradise is in the place I have said."[19]

Columbus's Last Experiences as Viceroy of the Indies

Columbus reached Santo Domingo on August 31, 1498. Again he returned to mutinous colonists and natives warring against them because of their cruelty. His brothers, Bartolomé and Diego, had failed to keep order, and one of their lieutenants, Francisco Roldán, had risen up against them.

Roldán had permitted the colonists to mistreat and overwork the natives and loot their villages. Roldán had also intercepted the three ships carrying provisions, and many of their convict-crews had joined the rebels. Fernando's biography of his father described the situation:

> Entering the city of Santo Domingo almost blind from his continual vigils, the Admiral hoped to rest after that difficult voyage and find his people at peace. But he found . . . all the families of the island [Hispaniola] infected with a . . . rebellious spirit. Part of the people he had left were dead, and of the survivors more than 160 were sick with the French sickness. Many had joined the rebel Roldán. Moreover the relief ships he had dispatched . . . had not arrived.

Fernando then related the background of this situation:

An Indescribable Service to God

Despite Las Casas's many complaints about the evils set in motion in the New World by Columbus, he indulged in this whole-hearted praise of Columbus, taken from History of the Indies.

"Many is the time I have wished that God would again inspire me and that I had Cicero's gift of eloquence to extol the indescribable service to God and to the whole world which Christopher Columbus rendered at the cost of such pain and dangers, such skill and expertise, when he so courageously discovered the New World. . . . Is there anything on earth comparable to opening the tightly shut doors of an ocean that no one dared enter before? And supposing someone in the most remote past did enter, the feat was so utterly forgotten as to make Columbus's discovery as arduous as if it had been the first time. But since it is obvious that at that time God gave this man the keys to the awesome seas, he and no other unlocked the darkness, to him and to no other is owed for ever and ever all that exists beyond those doors. He showed the way to the discovery of immense territories whose coastline today measures over 12,000 leagues from pole to pole and whose inhabitants form wealthy and illustrious nations of diverse peoples and languages. Their rites and customs differ but they all have in common the traits of simplicity, peacefulness, gentleness, and, of all the sons of Adam, they are without exception the most patient. In addition, they are eminently ready to be brought to the knowledge of their Creator and to the Faith."

Thirty months had elapsed since Columbus had left Hispaniola [March 1496, when he returned from his second voyage, to August 1498]. At first the people anticipated the Admiral's speedy return with relief . . . and remained fairly peaceful. But after the passage of a year, with provisions running short and sickness growing, they became discontented . . . and complained much. . . . There arose among them one who sought to stir them up and make himself head of a faction, Francisco Roldán. . . . For, said Roldán, the people knew how hardly and cruelly the Adelantado [Governor] treated them, forcing them to work in the fields and build forts; and since they had no hope of the Admiral's return with relief . . . [the Spanish settlers] should refuse to be ruled by a for-eigner [Columbus was an Italian] for wages that were never paid them, while they could be leading an easy and abundant life. All the wealth of the is-land should be equally divided among them, and they should be allowed to use the Indians as they pleased, . . . whereas now they might not even take for themselves any Indian women they pleased.[20]

Columbus solved the problem after long negotiations with Roldán by allowing those colonists who wished to return to Spain to do so free of cost. He also agreed to allow Roldán to be *alcalde,* "mayor," and entrusted him with important missions. Roldán served Columbus by helping to put down other rebel movements, but he continued to be a threat to law and order.

As soon as he was back in control, Columbus began to allot lands to Spanish settlers by a free land-grant system, the *repartimiento.* Along with pacifying Roldán, this measure helped to reduce, but by no means end, the turmoil in the colony. The *repartimiento,* however, refused land ownership to

The Cruelest People

Bartolomé de Las Casas describes Spanish atrocities in this excerpt from his History of the Indies. *In detailing Spanish behavior, Las Casas created what is known as the Black Legend; the charge that Spaniards were the cruelest people in Europe.*

The Indians have "only naked bellies to shield them from the Spaniards' mighty steel weapons, and only bows, poisonless arrows and stones . . . to use against the Spaniards. . . . It was a general rule among Spaniards to be cruel; not just cruel, but extraordinarily cruel so that harsh and bitter treatment would prevent Indians from daring to think of themselves as human beings or having a minute to think at all. So they would cut an Indian's hands and leave them dangling by a shred of skin. . . . They would test their swords and their manly strength on captured Indians and place bets on the slicing off of heads or the cutting of bod-ies in half with one blow. . . . [In one case], the Indians fought a while and fled but . . . they were unable to escape from their pursuers who captured some 700 men, gath-ered them in a house and stabbed them to death. . . . [This] is how the Spaniards avenged the eight Christians whom the Indians had had good reason to kill but a few days earlier. . . . My eyes have seen these acts so foreign to human nature, and now I tremble as I write, not believing them myself, afraid that perhaps I was dreaming. But truly this sort of thing has happened all over the Indies."

The Spanish were cruel to the native Americans in many cases. Here, they are forced to carry heavy loads for the Europeans, and those who are too slow are killed.

the natives. The Taínos were considered trespassers on land that had been their own country.

As Columbus again gained control of his colony, he was dealt a blow from Spain. In 1499 the Spanish government sent other explorers to the New World. In their minds, the business of exploration and discovery had to be speeded up, since England had now joined in the race for new

Amerigo Vespucci in the New World. The Italian explorer was sent by the Spanish crown to help claim the land Columbus had found.

overseas territories. Among the new explorers was the admiral's former captain, Alonso de Hojeda, and an Italian from Florence named Amerigo Vespucci, the man America was later named for.

In August 1500 Ferdinand and Isabella sent Francisco de Bobadilla to investigate the problems in Santo Domingo and to replace Columbus as governor. Bobadilla held a hearing at which many brought charges of misrule against Columbus. In a letter that October, Columbus complained of the way Bobadilla treated him:

> I ought to be judged as a captain who went from Spain to the Indies to conquer a numerous and warlike people, whose customs and religion are contrary to ours . . . and where, by the divine will, I have placed under the dominion of the King and Queen, our sovereigns, another world. . . . The Commander . . . took up his abode in my house, and just as he found it so he appropriated everything to himself. . . . About my papers I have a greater grievance, for he has completely deprived me of them.[21]

Also, in this letter, Columbus openly uses the word *conquer,* and the gentle Taínos had become *warlike* in his opinion. The situation had changed drastically since that first peaceful encounter of October 12, 1492.

Columbus Finds Rich Gold Mines but Returns to Spain in Chains

Bobadilla's arrival was a particularly cruel blow to Columbus because he had just received news that gold mines were finally found in the Cordillera mountains. Fernando wrote: "So many gold mines were discovered that all . . . went out prospecting for gold, paying the King a third of all they found."[22] Columbus wrote, in his letter of October 1500, "That day [around Christmas 1499] I learned there were eighty leagues of land and mines all over it."[23] He refers to "the good news about the gold" and complains that Bobadilla had arrived "now at the time when so much gold is found." The discovery did not change Bobadilla's mind, however: Columbus and his brother Diego were put in chains by Bobadilla and sent home.

Fernando wrote,

As soon as they had put out to sea, the skipper . . . offered to remove Columbus's chains, but he refused, saying he had been placed in chains in his Sovereigns' name . . . and he was resolved to keep those chains as a memorial of how well he had been rewarded for his many services. . . . On November 20, 1500, Columbus wrote the Sovereigns that he had arrived at Cadíz. As soon as they learned that he

Columbus was forced to return to Spain in chains after Bobadilla was given control of the American settlements.

came in chains, they ordered him set free and wrote expressing their good will toward him and their displeasure at Bobadilla's harsh treatment of him. They requested the Admiral to come to Court, assuring him that he would be treated with honor and his affairs settled with dispatch. . . . Bobadilla would be commanded to make restitution of the Admiral's property . . . and the rebels were to be tried and punished as their offenses deserved. Accordingly, the Sovereigns sent out Don Nicolás de Ovando [to replace Bobadilla]. At the same time . . . they resolved to dispatch the Admiral on another voyage from which they might derive some profit and with which he might be occupied only until Ovando had pacified the island of Hispaniola. . . . The Sovereigns made these promises because the Admiral had resolved to have nothing more to do with the affairs of the Indies.[24]

Native Slaves

Bartolomé de Las Casas created the Black Legend by means of stories such as these, from his History of the Indies. *The Black Legend was used by England to justify its seizing Spanish ships well into the seventeenth century. The other nations of Europe, however, often inflicted much worse evils on the native Americans that they controlled.*

The Spaniards "saw themselves as masters or lords, served and feared by tribes. . . . [Rather than] walking any distance . . . they rode the backs of Indians. . . . If they had more leisure, they traveled . . . on a hammock. . . . In this case they also had Indians carry large leaves to shade them from the sun and others to fan them with goose wings. I saw many an escort follow them loaded like a donkey with mining equipment and food. . . . Whenever they reached an Indian village, they consumed what to fifty Indians would represent abundance, and forced the chief to bring them whatever he had, to the accompaniment of dances. . . . They beat and insulted the Indians, hardly calling them anything but 'dog.' Would to God they treated them as such, because they would not have killed a dog in a million years, while they thought nothing of knifing Indians by tens and twenties and of cutting slices off them to test the sharpness of their blades. Two . . . Christians met two Indian boys one day, each carrying a parrot; they took the parrots and for fun beheaded the boys. . . . Another shot arrows into an Indian in public [because he failed] to deliver a letter with the speed he required."

The Fourth Voyage

On May 9, 1502, at age fifty-one, Columbus made what he called his "High Voyage." The monarchs' instructions to Columbus were to add new lands and wealth for the profit of Spain. Columbus left Cadiz with 140 men in four caravels. Among them were his thirteen-year-old son Fernando and his brother Bartolomé. Fernando later wrote that Columbus's mission was to find a way through the islands of Hispaniola and—finally—to the Indian Ocean. Columbus's voyage was in many ways his most difficult. All four ships were lost, he was shipwrecked on Jamaica for an entire year, a serious mutiny broke out, and thirty-two of the crewmen died.

As Columbus's ships passed near Santo Domingo on June 30, 1502, a storm endangered all lives aboard. Despite the royal command to avoid Santo Domingo, the admiral requested permission to land because of the approaching hurricane. He also warned Ovando not to launch the ships that were preparing to journey to Spain at that very moment. Ovando refused to allow Columbus into port and ignored Columbus's storm warnings. As a result, the fleet he sent out was nearly completely destroyed. Fernando's biography described the catastrophe:

> This fleet of 28 ships carried... Bobadilla, who had made prisoners of the Admiral and his brothers, Francisco Roldán, and all the other rebels who had done the Admiral so much hurt. God was pleased to close the eyes and minds of all those men so that they did not heed the Admiral's good advice. I am certain that this was Divine

Columbus's fourth voyage was plagued with misfortune. One of the difficulties was a serious mutiny.

This last statement was not quite accurate. Ferdinand and Isabella had *commanded* Columbus not to go to Santo Domingo and to stay out of political affairs there. The royal couple already knew about the gold rush in the Cordillera range and were pleased. In their letter to Columbus dated March 14, 1502, Ferdinand and Isabella again solemnly promised that all the titles and profits they had originally granted to him would be honored. However, it is clear from their actions that the monarchs had lost faith in Columbus as the man to govern their new colonies.

Columbus's ships were almost lost in a storm in June 1502. The situation was so desperate that the explorer even asked to land in Santo Domingo, which had been forbidden.

Providence, for had they arrived in Castile, they would never have been punished as their crimes deserved. . . . The flagship carrying Bobadilla and most of the rebels went down, and the storm did such havoc among the rest that only three or four ships weathered the tempest. This happened on the last day of June [1502].

A large shipment of gold and three hundred men were lost. Columbus weathered the storm and sailed on, although his ships were in bad repair. Fernando continued:

That is why the Admiral's enemies charged that by his magic arts he had raised the storm to take revenge on Bobadilla and his other enemies, seeing that not one of his four ships went down, while of [Bobadilla's] 28 . . . only one . . . reached Spain safely with 4,000 pesos of gold from the Admiral's revenues that his agent was bringing home. Three others that rode out the storm had to return to Santo Domingo in a battered and pitiful state.[25]

Soon after this event, natives told Columbus of gold in a place called Veragua, on the border of newly discovered Costa Rica and Panama. He also heard of the land of Ciguare to the west of Veragua, where people had luxurious clothing, great ships, horses, and trade fairs. Scholars think this may have been a description of the Aztec or Inca civilization. Columbus and his men reached Veragua and, indeed, found mines and collected more gold in two days than they had in four years on Hispaniola.

But recurring storms, wars against angry natives, and old sicknesses plagued the admiral. The ships were worm-eaten and taking in water. Yet Columbus says he was visited by the comforting voice of God: "Fear not; have trust; all these sufferings . . . have their reasons."[26]

By May 1, 1503, Columbus reached Jamaica. He was reduced to two ships that also took in so much water that they had to be abandoned. Columbus and the surviving crew of about a hundred men were marooned on Jamaica for more than a year before Ovando sent a ship to rescue them. During this time Columbus wrote his *Lettera Rarissima* [unique letter], which described his awful experience.

The Last Years and the Decline of Columbus's Fame

The Admiral of the Ocean Sea returned to Spain for the last time on November 7, 1504. Queen Isabella was terminally ill, so Columbus was almost totally ignored by the royal court. Six months after her death, King Ferdinand finally saw him—in May 1505. Columbus was extremely sickly, and his days of exploration were clearly behind him. Behind him too was the high esteem felt for him in Spain. Writers of Columbus's time were influenced by the news of dissension, warfare, sickness, and poverty that came from those who returned from the New World. Most of these evils had been blamed on Columbus himself.

As Columbus's reputation faded, those of the other explorers funded by the Spanish rulers grew. These men reaped the benefits of Columbus's early voyages. Capitalizing on Columbus's discovery of the Atlantic route, of the Cordillera gold mines, and of the newly realized pearls of Paria (South America), men such as Hojeda and Vespucci returned to Spain with large amounts of pearls and gold. Appreciation of their deeds filled people's conversations, and Columbus was almost forgotten.

The letters of Peter Martyr, one of the first European intellectuals to appreciate the importance of Columbus, reveal that Columbus's fame faded fast. Martyr's eight hundred letters were collected into a series of eight books called *Decadas de orbe novo (Decades Concerning the New World)*. Scholars have considered these letters as the first history of the Americas.

Martyr's *First Decade,* published in 1504, contributed to Columbus's fame. They described his first three voyages. Martyr interviewed the admiral every chance he got, though he himself never crossed the Atlantic. As each successive explorer returned, however, Martyr excitedly wrote about the latest news, and the name of Columbus retreated into the background.

Settlers found pearls in South America, but the discovery of riches came too late to restore Columbus's reputation.

This map of Hispaniola was published by Peter Martyr, who wrote of Columbus's discoveries.

Another factor in the eclipse of Columbus as a popular hero was the publication of Amerigo Vespucci's letters in 1503. He, too, was an explorer from Italy in the employ of Spain and Portugal. He had made at least two voyages, one with Hojeda and one navigating hundreds of miles down the coast of South America under the Portuguese flag. Vespucci's letters highlighted his exciting experiences in the New World.

Martin Waldseemüller drew this map based on the letters of Amerigo Vespucci. He labeled the area of Brazil America.

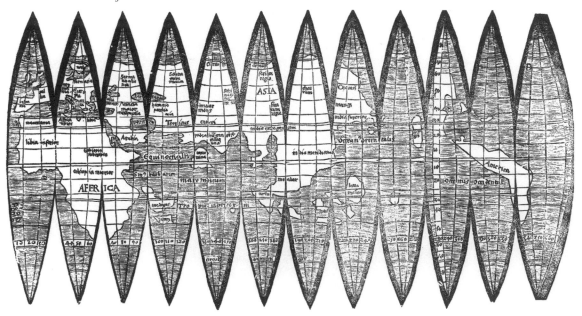

Columbus died in 1506, forgotten by his supporters. His death was not publicly acknowledged anywhere.

They were written in a lively style and made Columbus's exploits seem dim.

Columbus died on May 20, 1506, in Valladolid, in the heart of Castile. His death was not noticed publicly in Spain or anywhere else. The earliest reference to his death appeared ten years later in one of Martyr's *Decades*. It was very matter-of-fact:

Columbus being now departed from this life, the king began to take care how those lands may be inhabited with Christians to the increase of our faith.[27]

In the year following Columbus's death, a geography book based on Vespucci's letters was published in Lorraine, France. It was illustrated with a map drawn by Martin Waldseemüller, a German *cartographer* (map maker). The map was labeled "A Map of the World According to the Traditions of Ptolemy and the Voyages of Americus Vespucius," and it bore portraits of Ptolemy facing east and Vespucci facing west. The name *America* appeared in the area of Brazil in South America. By 1538, the name was applied to both American continents, while at the same time the name of Christopher Columbus was forgotten or unknown in the rest of Europe. An examination of Columbus's accomplishments would be left to future historians.

Chapter

6 The Mixed Legacy of Christopher Columbus

Christopher Columbus's importance to the world he lived in, to history, and to today's world continues to be evaluated. Because he was the first European to open the New World to colonization and exploitation, all of his writings, actions, and attitudes continue to be examined. Scholars believe that in many ways Columbus set the tone for later explorations of the New World. But how much responsibility Columbus should bear for what came after him remains a matter of debate. For a

Although Christopher Columbus brought the New and Old Worlds together, the meaning of his legacy continues to be debated.

biographer of Columbus, these matters deserve attention because they are all part of an evaluation of the man.

The voyages of Columbus resulted in an exchange of products and in an encounter of the people of two hemispheres. The result was that the entire world—both the old and the new—was changed by Columbus. Kirkpatrick Sale, in *Conquest of Paradise*, describes medieval Europe and how these voyages changed European attitudes:

> In the dark twilight of fifteenth-century Europe, the overriding question . . . was how to survive the misery and suffering and violence that seemed to be rushing the world to its end. The answer that came . . . was [Columbus's] conquest of paradise. . . . [Columbus began] the process by which Europe was able, eventually, to overcome its own desperate frailties and terrors, and find not only gold and silver and precious ores beyond imagining, not only foods that would sustain its population for centuries, . . . not only drugs it would take into its pharmacopoeia [available medicines] . . . not only vast resources of timber and furs and hides and water power, but the huge continent on which the people of Europe would spread themselves and their culture.[28]

Deception

Native American culture in the islands was different from European culture. Fernando's biography quotes Columbus about native leaders, both caciques and medicine men, deceiving the people under their control.

"Our people learned many other things having to do with their customs. . . . Beginning with their religion, I shall cite here the Admiral's own words:

'Each of their kings . . . has a house . . . used only for the service of the carved wooden images called *cemies*. . . . In these houses there is a . . . wooden dish, in which is kept a powder. . . . Then, through a cane having two branches that they insert in the nose, they sniff up this powder. . . . [It] makes them lose their senses and rave like drunken men. . . . It once happened that some Christians entered such a house . . . and the *cemi* gave a loud cry and spoke in their language, from which it became clear that the statue was . . . hollow, and to the lower part was attached a . . . trumpet . . . connected to a dark side of the house, . . . where was hidden a person who said whatever the cacique wanted him to say. . . . The Spaniards . . . kicked the *cemi* over, finding what was described above. Seeing that his ruse was discovered, the cacique earnestly pleaded with us to say nothing . . . because it was by means of that deception that he kept [his subjects] in obedience to him.'"

Columbus's impact on the mind of Europe was immense. Historian William H. Prescott writes:

It was not the gradual acquisition of some border territory, a province or a kingdom that had been gained, but a New World that was now thrown open to the Europeans. The races of animals, the mineral treasures, the vegetable forms, and the varied aspects of nature, man in the different phases of civilization, filled the mind with entirely new sets of ideas, that changed the habitual current of thought and stimulated it to indefinite conjecture. . . . It was a world of romance that was thrown open.[29]

In the minds of Europeans, the Atlantic Ocean was no longer mysterious and forbidding, but the road to wealth.

In the realm of agricultural exchange, Europe received more from the Americas than it gave. Native American agriculture contributed tomatoes, potatoes, sweet potatoes, squash, pumpkins, almost all the kinds

New World Medicine

In this passage from Fernando's biography of Columbus, Spanish priest Padre Ramon describes the medical practices of the native Americans.

"The following account [is] by Fray Ramon, who knew their language and was charged by me to set down all their rites and antiquities: . . . How the buhuitihus practice medicine . . . and the deceptions they practice in their cures. . . . When an Indian falls ill, they bring [in] the buhuitihu. . . . [He] takes some small bones and a little meat . . . and puts it in his mouth. . . . Entering the sick man's hut, . . . he goes toward the sick man, . . . and walks about him twice. . . . Then he . . . takes him by the legs, . . . after which he draws his hands away forcefully, as if pulling something out. Then he goes to the door, shuts it, and speaks to it, saying: 'Begone to the mountain . . . or where you will'; . . . then he sucks at the sick man's neck, or stomach, . . . or some other part of the body. Having done this, he begins to cough and make a face as if he had eaten something bitter; then he spits into his hand the stone or bone or piece of meat that he put in his mouth at home. . . . And if it is a piece of food, he tells the sick man, 'You have eaten something that caused the sickness. . . . See how I have taken it out of your body, where your *cemi* lodged it because you did not pray to him or build him a shrine.'"

Native healers, or buhuitihus, *tend to sick patients.*

*The native Americans culti-
vated and smoked tobacco,
one of the many crops taken
back to Europe from America.*

of beans, peanuts, pecans, hickory nuts, black walnuts, sunflower seeds, cranberries, blueberries, strawberries, pineapple, maple syrup, artichokes, peppers, chocolate, vanilla, allspice, sassafras, avocados, and maize (corn). All of these foods were completely unknown outside of the Americas in 1492. Of American animals, the greatest contribution to Europe was the turkey. Native American civil rights leader LaDonna Harris notes,

> Because native peoples did not have written documents, many of their contributions are not well known. . . . Foods that are considered ethnic foods of Europe actually came from this continent. They . . . revolutionized the food chain of the world. Also the wealth that came from this hemisphere—the gold and silver, the tobacco, cotton and sugar crops—changed the entire economic structure of Europe: from serfdom into industry. It is ironic that the wealth which came from the Indian people was so detrimental to them.[30]

Historian William McNeill attributes Europe's ability to dominate the world to the American potato. Since potatoes produced four times more calories per acre than Old World rye,

> This meant that across the vast plain of northern Europe four times as many people could live on the produce of the soil when they learned to eat potatoes instead of rye bread. . . . It is no exaggeration to say that the swift rise of industrial Germany [in the late nineteenth century] was the greatest political monument to the impact of American food crops on Europe—and on other continents as well, for World Wars I and II were among the consequences of that rise.

American crops caused and supported rapid European population growth. McNeill continues with a statement that applies to both Europe and America:

> The flood of emigrants [from Europe] who peopled the Americas and other lands overseas could not have survived

infancy without the extra calories that came from potatoes and maize.[31]

Potatoes and corn became basic global foods. These food crops provide about 35 percent of China's food supply, and China produces about three-fourths of the world's sweet potatoes. William McNeill concludes that these foods are "by far the greatest treasure that the Old World acquired from the New."

Columbus's Impact on the New World

Columbus's impact was just as vast on the New World as it was on the Old. In attempting to remake Spain in the New World, the Spaniards radically changed the ecology of the new land. European plants enriched the agricultural landscape—peach, pear,

---

Native Genocide

In this excerpt from his History of the Indies, *Bartolomé de Las Casas discusses the population of the islands first encountered by Columbus.*

"As Christopher Columbus informed the King, it is a fact that innumerable people inhabited this land, and the Archbishop of Seville, Diego de Deza, told me one day that he had heard the Admiral mention he counted a million and 100,000 heads. This must have referred only to the people in the vicinity of the Cibao mines on whom he had imposed a gold tribute per capita, . . . and perhaps he included in this number part of the Xaraguá province which paid tribute in cassava and raw and spun cotton. I think without fear of erring too far that there lived more than three million people on this island [Hispaniola], because a number of areas had not yet been explored."

In Las Casas's shorter book, The Devastation of the Indies: A Brief Account, *he complains about the depletion of the native population of San Juan and Jamaica.*
"Before the arrival of the Spaniards there had lived on these islands more than six hundred thousand souls, it has been stated. I believe there were more than one million inhabitants, and now, in each of the two islands, there are no more than two hundred persons, all the others having perished without the Faith and without the holy sacraments."

---

apple, olive, orange, and lemon trees; grains (wheat, rice, and oats), chick-peas, grape vines, melons, onions, radishes, turnips, cabbage, and sugar cane.

The Spaniards also cut down great numbers of trees for fuel and construction. The loss of the dense tree cover caused changes in the landscape, and the resulting reduction of the tropical rain forest may even have influenced the climate by turning lush forests into deserts. Moreover, European animals—horses, cattle, pigs, and sheep—grazed the land and stripped ground covers. The Spaniards saw these vast changes as improvements to the land, making it productive and useful. These attitudes toward the land greatly contrasted with those of the native Americans. As Kirkpatrick Sale notes about the Europeans:

> It was right and "natural" . . . to fell trees, clear brush, "recover" fens and marshes, till soils, plant crops, graze herds, harness beasts, kill predators and "vermin," dig canals and ditches, and in general make use of the bounty of nature that a benevolent Lord had provided for them.[32]

The raising of these plants and animals fed the ever-growing population of the New World. Pigs especially multiplied rapidly: a load of thirteen pigs brought from Europe increased to seven hundred in three years, and to fifteen thousand in sixteen years.

Columbus's Impact on the Native American Population

The greatest change of all in the New World after the arrival of the Europeans was the reduction in the native population, from millions to a few thousand.

Many native Americans were tortured and killed by cruel, conquering Spaniards.

Bartolomé de Las Casas, who was on Columbus's second voyage, estimated that three million Taíno people lived on Hispaniola when Columbus arrived in 1492. In 1542, Las Casas reported that only two hundred Taínos were still alive. Twenty years later the Taínos were extinct.

Many natives died at the hands of the Spaniards. Las Casas reported in his *History of the Indies* almost unbelievably cruel treatment:

> It was a general rule among Spaniards to be cruel; not just cruel, but extraordinarily cruel so that harsh and bitter treatment would prevent Indians from daring to think of themselves as human beings or having a minute to think at all. So they would cut an Indian's

hands and leave them dangling by a shred of skin and they would send him on. . . . They would test their swords and their manly strength on captured Indians and place bets on the slicing off of heads or the cutting of bodies in half with one blow.[33]

Native deaths were not caused directly by conquest alone. The vast majority of natives died from new strains of European germs. Eyewitnesses of the ravages of these diseases said the natives "died like fish in a pail." Native Americans had almost no immunity to the new viruses, microbes, and bacteria carried by Columbus's crews. These infectious diseases include smallpox, measles, whooping cough, malaria, yellow fever, diphtheria, typhus, and flu. Of these, smallpox, first

---

Appreciating Native American Culture

Philip Tajitsu Nash, professor at City University of New York Law School, and civil rights leader Emilienne Ireland contribute several insights in their article "Rethinking Terminology," in Rethinking Columbus.

"Nor can traditional Native American life be called 'simple' or 'primitive' in an intellectual sense. A typical elder of the Wauja people in the Amazon rain forest, for example, has memorized hundreds of sacred songs and stories; plays several musical instruments; and knows the habits and habitats of hundreds of forest animals, birds, and insects, as well as the medicinal uses of local plants. He can guide his sons in building a two-story tall house using only axes, machetes, and materials from the forest. He is an expert agronomist. He speaks several languages fluently; knows precisely how he is related to several hundred of his closest kin."

These authors caution students to be alert for terms that suggest that native Americans were inferior to the Europeans.
"'Civilizing' or 'Christianizing' a people presumes that their own society and religion are inferior. Calling the European conquerors 'courageous' or 'far-sighted' justifies their actions. Saying that European atrocities in the Western Hemisphere were 'unavoidable' (or that the perpetrators of genocide were only 'products of their time') dulls our sense of injustice regarding events both past and present."

The Spaniards tried to use native American labor to grow their crops in America, but the native population was not large enough. Instead, the Spaniards were forced to import slaves from Africa.

identified in America in 1518, was the worst killer.

An Aztec historian trained in the Roman alphabet in the sixteenth century described the impact of smallpox on his people. The disease spared the Europeans but

> spread over the [native] people as great destruction. Some it quite covered [with pustules] on all parts—their faces, their heads, their breasts, and so on. . . . They could not move; they could not stir; they could not change

position, nor lie on one side, nor face down, nor on their backs. . . . Covered with pustules, very many people died of them.

Another Aztec wrote about the time before the coming of the Spaniards:

> There was then no sickness; they had no aching bones; they had then no high fever; they had then no smallpox; they had then no burning chest; they had then no abdominal pain; they had

Slaves were shipped across the Atlantic from Africa to help grow labor-intensive crops like sugar in the New World.

then no consumption; they had then no headache. At that time the course of humanity was orderly. The foreigners made it otherwise when they arrived here.[34]

The germs traveled ahead of the Europeans. By the time Francisco Pizarro reached the Incas in 1532, they had suffered a horrible outbreak of smallpox, and he had an easy time conquering them. Ten years later Hernando de Soto, who had been with Pizarro, found empty villages and death houses full of drying cadavers in the area now known as Georgia: proof of prior epidemic. It has been estimated that diseases destroyed up to 90 percent of those native populations who died in Mesoamerica after the coming of the Spaniards.

Columbus's Impact on Africa

The widespread deaths of the native people had a far-reaching impact. Because the natives were vulnerable to disease and their numbers were declining, Europeans needed to find a new source of cheap labor to help them turn the New World into what they hoped would be a burgeoning European colony.

In particular, the sugar cane root that Columbus brought from the Canary Islands to Hispaniola required native labor. Sugar is a labor-intensive crop that requires many hours to harvest. The native Americans died in droves from overwork while working this crop. To continue cultivating sugar, Columbus and later Europeans looked to Africa for a source of labor.

The first enslaved Africans arrived in the New World in 1505. Jack Weatherford, a scholar of early American history, writes:

By 1519 the Spaniards had nearly exhausted the supply of Indian slaves in the Caribbean. [In] a letter from that year . . . Diego [Columbus], the son of Christopher, beseeched King Charles V of Spain for permission to import African slaves to replace the depleted supply of Indians. This letter reveals the earliest known official request to import Africans, and with the elegant strokes on that page began three centuries of the cruel commerce across the mid-Atlantic.

The impact of slavery on Africans was one of the most unfortunate legacies of

An Incomparable Holocaust

Chief Billy Redwing Tayac, hereditary chief of Piscataway people, summarized the feelings of native Americans about their bad treatment by Europeans in "Interview with Chief Tayac: Struggles Unite Native Peoples," in Rethinking Columbus.

"Nowhere in the annals of history has there been a repetition of what has occurred here. The Europeans invaded all our land . . . and tried their best to destroy a race of people and their cultures and religions. It is a holocaust that cannot be compared to anything else in the history of humanity. Even today, in the 20th Century, Indian people are not considered a part of mankind. . . . In the United Nations, all other races of people—black, white and yellow—are represented. Red people have no voice. If atrocities occur against us, we . . . have to go to the oppressor government . . . to voice our concerns. This would be a like a Jew going to Hitler to express his concerns about the horrible extermination policies directed towards his people in the 1940's. . . . When the Nazis occupied France during World War II, those who opposed them were called 'freedom fighters'. . . . When Sioux warriors defeated United States warriors at Little Big Horn in 1876, the popular press called it a 'massacre.' However, when the United States cavalry machine-gunned unarmed men, women and children at Wounded Knee in 1890 . . . more Congressional Medals of Honor were given there than in any previous battle. This feeling of being outside the American government has its roots in the fact that we are a sovereign people who were here thousands of years before Columbus."

A Legacy of Devastation and Crime

Columbus has been criticized in recent biographies. An example comes from John Noble Wilford, "Discovering Columbus," published in the New York Times Magazine, *August 11, 1991.*

"Columbus left his new world a legacy of devastation and crime. He might have been an unselfish promoter of geographical science; he proved a rabid seeker for gold. . . . He might have won converts to the fold of Christ by the kindness of his spirit; . . . He might, like Las Casas, have rebuked the fiendishness of his contemporaries; he set them an example of perverted belief. . . . In time, Las Casas forced his contemporaries to question the morality of the brutal treatment of the Indians at the hands of Columbus and his successors. . . . It is time that the encounter be viewed not only from the European standpoint, but from that of the indigenous Americans. . . . [Columbus] goaded the native Taínos into bloody rebellion. Thousands of Taínos were raped, killed, and tortured and their villages burned. . . . The only example Columbus set was one of pettiness, self-aggrandizement and a lack of magnanimity. . . . Was he a great man? No, if greatness is measured by one's stature among contemporaries. . . . Yes, if greatness derives from the audacity of his undertaking . . . and the magnitude of its impact on subsequent history."

Columbus's voyages. In a short time, African slaves replaced Indians as slave labor. Weatherford even calls Columbus the first slave monger:

> Indian slavery prepared most parts of North America for colonization. Christopher Columbus started this practice by kidnapping twenty-five Indians whom he took back to Spain with him as slaves. A few years later, when he was pressed to make a profit from his voyages, and had found little gold or spices with which to do so, he began shipping Caribbean Indians back to Spain to be sold in the Portuguese Azores, the Spanish Canaries, and the markets of Seville. . . . Columbus pursued a deliberate policy of using Indian slavery and Indian labor to finance the conquest of the new lands. Within the first decade of Columbus's arrival, the Spaniards had shipped out at least three thousand Indian slaves, and possibly as many as six thousand, to Seville.[35]

Many far-reaching changes have been laid at the feet of Christopher Columbus. Depending on interpretation, Columbus has been directly responsible for such current troubles as the oppression of native-American and African-American peoples, the destruction of the environment, and the leveling of natives by disease.

This interpretation of Columbus is far different from the traditional one. In the past, Columbus was viewed as a hero, a singular individual who bravely sailed into unknown waters. And surely, Columbus should still be credited with changing European knowledge of the world and paving the way for European immigrants to find a way toward freedom from the rigid social structure and poverty in which they lived.

More important than these current reevaluations, however, is the fact that the last words on Columbus have yet to be written. Five hundred years have passed, and the impact of Columbus's journeys continues to be interpreted. In the end, Columbus's legacy is widespread and goes far beyond his own lifetime. The reexamination of Columbus is, in a way, a reexamination of all of us, white and black, native American and European. It is an examination of the prejudices, the attitudes, and the legacies that continue to pervade our society.

Notes

Editor's note: Some of the citations for quotes in the text have been combined to avoid undue repetition. If a quote is uncited, the next citation applies.

Introduction: Toward a Balanced View of Columbus

1. Daniel Boorstin, *The Discoverers.* New York: Random House, 1983.

Chapter 1: Columbus: Early Life

2. Björn Landström, *Columbus.* New York: Macmillan, 1967.
3. Landström, *Columbus.*

Chapter 2: The Age of Columbus: Europe in 1492

4. Boorstin, *The Discoverers.*
5. Benjamin Keen, tr., *The Life of the Admiral Christopher Columbus by His Son Ferdinand.* New Brunswick, NJ: Rugters University Press, 1959.
6. John Noble Wilford, *The Mysterious History of Columbus.* New York: Knopf, 1991.

Chapter 3: The First Voyage

7. Keen, *The Life.*
8. Landström, *Columbus.*
9. Keen, *The Life.*
10. E. G. Bourne, *The Northmen, Columbus, and Cabot, 985–1503.* New York: Barnes and Noble, 1967.
11. Bourne, *The Northmen.*
12. Bourne, *The Northmen.*
13. Kirkpatrick Sale, *The Conquest of Paradise.* New York: Alfred A. Knopf, 1990.

Chapter 4: The Second Voyage

14. Keen, *The Life.*
15. Sale, *The Conquest of Paradise.*
16. Keen, *The Life.*
17. Keen, *The Life.*

Chapter 5: Columbus's Last Voyages

18. Bourne, *The Northmen.*
19. Cecil Jane, *The Four Voyages of Columbus.* New York: Dover, 1961.
20. Keen, *The Life.*
21. Jane, *The Four Voyages.*
22. Keen, *The Life.*
23. Sale, *The Conquest.*
24. Keen, *The Life.*
25. Keen, *The Life.*
26. Bourne, *The Northmen.*
27. Sale, *The Conquest.*

Chapter 6: The Mixed Legacy of Christopher Columbus

28. Sale, *The Conquest.*
29. William H. Prescott, *History of the Conquest of Mexico and History of the Conquest of Peru.* New York: Modern Library, 1936.
30. LaDonna Harris, "If I Had Five Minutes to Spend with Students. . . . " in *Rethinking Columbus,* Bill Bigelow et al, eds. Milwaukee, WI: Rethinking Schools, 1992.
31. William H. McNeill, "American Food Crops in the Old World," in Herman J. Viola and Carolyn Margolis, eds., *Seeds of Change.* Washington and London: Smithsonian Institution Press, 1991.
32. Sale, *The Conquest.*
33. Andrée Collard, tr., *Bartolomé de Las Casas: History of the Indies.* New York: Harper and Row, 1971.
34. Alfred W. Crosby, *The Columbian Exchange.* Westport, CT: Greenwood Press, 1972.
35. Jack Weatherford, *Native Roots: How the Indians Enriched America.* New York: Crown, 1991.

For Further Reading

Author's note: All of the following works about Christopher Columbus are entertaining, informative, and worthwhile. Most are available at public libraries.

Bill Bigelow et al., eds. Special issue *Rethinking Columbus,* January–February 1992. Available from Rethinking Schools, 1001 E. Keefe Ave., Milwaukee, WI 53212. Bigelow is a leading opponent of Columbus and sees only evil resulting from Columbus's arrival in the New World.

E. G. Bourne, ed., *The Northmen, Columbus, and Cabot, 985–1503.* New York: Barnes and Noble, 1967. Provides good translations of key documents in Columbus's life. Commentaries are based on the actual documents.

Herma Briffault, tr., *Bartolomé de Las Casas: The Devastation of the Indies, A Brief Account.* New York: Seabury, 1980. This summary of Las Casas's work focuses on the issue of Spanish atrocities.

Andrée Collard, tr., *Bartolomé de Las Casas: History of the Indies.* New York: Harper and Row, 1971. With Fernando's *Life of Columbus,* Las Casas's *History* is the best original and contemporary appraisal of Columbus.

Alfred W. Crosby, *The Columbian Exchange.* Westport, CT: Greenwood Press, 1972. This book provides the best treatment of the ongoing medical, cultural, biosocial, and sociopolitical meaning of the exchanges between Europe and the Americas. Crosby covers the exchange of diseases.

The Economist, "In Defence of Columbus," December 21, 1991–January 3, 1992. A strenuous defense of Columbus.

Felipe Fernandez-Armesto, *Columbus.* New York: Oxford University Press, 1991. This book takes one of the most objective approaches to Columbus. Armesto describes a real human being, one placed in a crucial role in a situation unique in history, striving to overcome obstacles of his own mistakes and those of his men. Armesto judges Columbus neither as hero nor villain.

Cecil Jane, *The Four Voyages of Columbus.* New York: Dover, 1961. Provides good translations of key documents on Columbus's life and voyages. Introductory essays are excellent. This volume is also currently available in paperback.

Benjamin Keen, tr., *The Life of the Admiral Christopher Columbus by His Son Ferdinand.* New Brunswick, NJ: Rutgers University Press, 1959. Ferdinand's biography of his father is an important reference for the life and thought of Columbus.

Björn Landström, *Columbus.* New York: Macmillan, 1967. This book is attractively illustrated by the author. It provides the story of Columbus in clear and easy-to-understand language, aided by clear illustrations and maps. It is very good at providing information on ships and maritime instruments of the time.

Eugene Lyon, "Search for Columbus," *National Geographic,* January 1992. This article covers Columbus's early life in Genoa and his identity as a Genoese citizen.

Newsweek: Columbus Special Issue, Fall–Winter 1991. This issue contains articles about most Columbus topics. Well balanced, it is useful to students.

William H. Prescott, *History of the Conquest of Mexico and History of the Conquest of Peru.* New York: Modern Library, 1936. This is the classic and definitive treatment of Spain's conquests of Aztecs and Incas. It covers the period immediately following the arrival of Columbus.

Kirkpatrick Sale, *The Conquest of Paradise.* New York: Alfred A. Knopf, 1990. This volume contains a great deal of information, but it is not well organized. Sale has provided the classic negative view of Columbus, suggesting that every evil in history since 1492 is Columbus's fault. Still, it is a most interesting book to read, even when Sale draws unfair conclusions from the available information.

Simon Schama, "Circus 1492: Who the Admiral Was and Who He Wasn't. They All Laughed at Christopher Columbus," *The New Republic,* January 6–13, 1992. This article comments at length on the National Gallery exhibit, "Circa 1492," which largely ignored Columbus the person. It follows with a fairly negative assessment of the Admiral.

Peter Schrag, *The European Mind and the Discovery of A New World.* Boston: D. C. Heath, 1965. This book is a collection of original quotations that focus on Europe's knowledge of the geography of the world, from ancient writers to the time of Columbus.

John Boyd Thacher, *Christopher Columbus, His Life, His Work, His Remains.* New York: G. P. Putnam's Sons, 1903. These three massive volumes have furnished British and American scholars with much of the information they have been able to use in the rash of Columbus books that have appeared in 1991 and 1992. Thacher has provided many hard-to-find documents in the original language and in English translations. He has important chapters on Peter Martyr, Las Casas, and other early reporters of Columbus's career. The volumes can be found in some college libraries.

Herman J. Viola and Carolyn Margolis, eds., *Seeds of Change.* Washington and London: Smithsonian Institution Press, 1991. This is a valuable collection of articles by different writers. Articles cover the transfer of ideas, animal species, foods, and diseases from Europe to America and from America to Europe.

Jack Weatherford, *Native Roots: How the Indians Enriched America.* New York: Crown Publishers, 1991. This is an important book for describing the many native American accomplishments that were adopted by Europeans and those that were not.

Delno West and August Kling, trs. and commentary, *The Libro de las Profecías of Christopher Columbus.* Gainesville, FL: University of Florida Press, 1991. This volume contains the original Spanish and Latin and English translation of the prophecies Columbus collected. The authors' introductory chapter on Columbus's intellectual background highlights the large part that religion played in his overall philosophy of life.

John Noble Wilford, *The Mysterious History of Columbus.* New York: Alfred A. Knopf, 1991. This book contains comments on more Columbus questions than most other excellent books. If one book on Columbus must be selected, this is perhaps the most valuable reference to keep handy.

Works Consulted

Silvio Bedini, *The Christopher Columbus Encyclopedia.* New York: Simon and Schuster Academic Reference, 1991.

Daniel Boorstin, *The Discoverers.* New York: Random House, 1983.

Michael Coe, Dean Snow, Elizabeth Benson, *Atlas of Ancient America.* New York: Facts on File, 1988.

Kathleen A. Deagon, "Europe's First Foothold in the New World: La Isabela," *National Geographic,* Vol. 181, No. 1.

Oliver C. Dunn and James E. Kelley, *The Diario of Christopher Columbus's First Voyage to America: 1492–1493.* Norman: Oklahoma University Press, 1987.

John Dyson, *Columbus: For Gold, God, and Glory.* New York: Simon and Schuster, 1991.

Juan Friede and Benjamin Keen, *Bartolomé de Las Casas in History.* DeKalb: Northern Illinois University Press, 1971.

Robert H. Fuson, tr., *The Log of Christopher Columbus.* Camden, ME: International Marine Publishing, 1987.

Stephen Greenblatt, *Marvelous Possessions: The Wonder of the New World.* Chicago: University of Chicago Press, 1991.

Lewis Hanke, *The Spanish Struggle for Justice in the Conquest of America.* Boston: Little, Brown and Company, 1965.

Joachim Leithäuser, *Worlds Beyond the Horizon.* New York: Alfred A. Knopf, 1955.

Barnet Litvinoff, *Fourteen Ninety Two: The Decline of Medievalism and the Rise of the Modern Age.* New York: Charles Scribner's Sons, 1991.

William H. McNeill, "American Food Crops in the Old World," in Herman J. Viola and Carolyn Margolis, eds., *Seeds of Change.* Washington and London: Smithsonian Institution Press, 1991.

Jerald T. Milanich and Susan Milbrath, eds., *First Encounters: Spanish Explorations in the Caribbean and the United States, 1492–1570.* Gainesville: University of Florida Press, 1989.

Samuel Eliot Morison, *Admiral of the Ocean Sea: A Life of Christopher Columbus.* Boston: Little, Brown and Company, 1991.

———, *The European Discovery of America.* New York: Oxford University Press, 1971–1974.

George E. Nunn, *The Geographical Conceptions of Columbus.* New York: American Geographical Society, 1924.

J. H. Parry, *The Age of Reconnaissance.* New York: Mentor, 1963.

———, *The Establishment of the European Hegemony 1415–1715.* New York: Harper Torchbook, 1949.

Boies Penrose, *Travel and Discovery in the Renaissance, 1420–1620.* Cambridge, MA: Harvard University Press, 1952.

Jeffrey Burton Russell, *Inventing the Flat Earth: Columbus and Modern Historians.* New York: Praeger, 1991.

Jeremy A. Sabloff, *The Cities of Ancient Mexico: Reconstructing a Lost World.* New York: Thames and Hudson, 1989.

J. Oliver Thomson, *History of Ancient Geography.* New York: Biblo and Tannen, 1965.

D. W. Waters, *The Art of Navigation in England in Elizabethan and Early Stuart Times.* New Haven, CT: Yale University Press, 1958.

———, "Early Time and Distance Measurement at Sea," *Journal of the Institute of Navigation,* Vol. 8, 1955.

P. Watts, "Prophecy and Discovery: On the Spiritual Origins of Christopher Columbus's 'Enterprise of the Indies,'" *American Historical Review,* Vol. 90, No. 1.

Index

Africa, impact of Columbus, 84–87
agriculture, New World's contribution to, 77, 79–90
Aguado, Juan, 58–59
Alfonso, king of Portugal, 25
Alvarez Chanca, Diego, 53
America, first appearance of name, 75
Arana, Diego de, 51
Aristotle, 26
astrolabe, 29
Aztecs, 72, 83–84

Biblioteca Colombina, 22
black Americans
    impact of Columbus on, 7–8
    slavery of, 84–87
Black Legend, 67, 70
Bobadilla, Francisco de, 68–72
Bohio (Hispaniola), 40–43
The Book of Prophecies (Columbus), 64
Boorstin, Daniel, 8, 21, 24
Bourne, E. G., 18, 40, 41, 46, 63
buhuitihus, 78

Cabot, John, 60–61
Cabral, Pedro, 62–63
Caonabó, 51, 57–59
cartography, 21
Charles V, king of Spain, 85
Charles VIII, king of France, 19
Chrysoloras, Manuel, 21
Colba (Cuba), 39–40, 54–55

Colon, Cristóbal. *See* Columbus, Christopher
Columbus, Bartolomé (brother of Columbus), 9–10, 16, 19, 54, 57, 60, 65, 71
Columbus, Bianchinetta (sister of Columbus), 9
Columbus, Christopher
    Africa, impact by Columbus, 84–87
    on available gold, 53
    The Book of Prophecies, 64
    Cuba, exploration of, 54–55
    defense of his acts, 68
    first sighting of land, 34–35
    as first slave monger, 86–87
    first, triumphant return, 43–46
    Garden of Eden, 63–64
    gold as motivator, 52–53
    Lettera Rarissima, 63, 72
    as map maker and bookseller, 10, 15
    marriage(s), 11
    "Memorial on the Settlement and Government", 46
    mixed legacy of, 76–86
    natives
        attitudes toward, 41–42
        Columbus blamed for problems, 64
        description of, 36–38
        impact on population, 81–84

    near-mutiny and, 33, 35, 43
    shipwrecked and marooned, 71–72
    skill as navigator, 32–33
    voyages
        first, 31–43
        second, 48–59
        third, 62–69
        fourth, 71–72
    wrote will, 61
Columbus, Diego (brother of Columbus), 9, 12–13, 54, 56, 65, 69
Columbus, Diego (son of Columbus), 11, 18, 57, 60, 85
Columbus, Domenico (father of Columbus), 9
Columbus, Fernando (son of Columbus), 11
    biography of father, 11, 17, 22, 26, 31–36, 38, 51, 55, 61, 65–67, 77, 78
Columbus (Fernandez-Armesto), 42, 50, 55
compass, 29–30, 33
Conquest of Paradise (Sale), 76
Cordillera and gold, 71, 73
Cosmos (Sagan), 28
Cuba (Colba), 39–40, 54–55
Cuneo, Michele de, 32, 52–53, 57

d'Ailly, Pierre, 22
Decades Concerning the New World (Martyr), 73, 75

The Devastation of the Indies (Las Casas), 80
Deza, Diego de, 80
Dias, Bartholomeu, 16
"Discovering Columbus" (Wilford), 86
diseases, 49, 82–84

encomienda, 59
Enríquez de Arana, Beatríz, 15, 60
Eratosthenes, 28

al-Farghani, 10, 23
Ferdinand, king of Spain
  contract with Columbus, 18–19
  final meeting with Columbus, 73
  greets triumphant Columbus, 45
  keeps Columbus waiting, 12–15, 17
  specific orders for Columbus, 62, 71
Fernandez-Armesto, Felipe, 42, 50, 55
Fontanarossa, Susanna (mother of Columbus), 9

Gama, Vasco da, 60–61
Geography (Ptolemy), 21
Guacanagarí, *kaseka* of Hispaniola, 41, 51, 58
Guanahaní (San Salvador), 35

Harris, LaDonna, 79
Henry the Navigator, 26
High Voyage, 71
Hispaniola (Bohio), 40–43, 74
History of the Indies (Las Casas), 25, 28, 40, 45, 52, 58, 60, 64, 66, 67, 70, 80, 81–82

History of the World (Pius II), 22
Hojeda, Alonso de, 58, 60, 68, 73–74

Incas, 72, 84
Ireland, Emilienne, 82
Isabela (settlement), 51–54, 56–57
Isabella, queen of Spain
  contract with Columbus, 18–19
  death, 73
  greets triumphant Columbus, 45
  keeps Columbus waiting, 12–15, 17
  slaves, forbade taking of, 57
  specific orders for Columbus, 62
Island of the Seven Cities, 25–27

John II, king of Portugal, 12, 16, 43

Kublai Khan, 24, 27

La Navidad, 42–43
  massacre at, 50–51
Landström, Björn, 20
Las Casas, Bartolomé de
  The Devastation of the Indies, 80
  History of the Indies, 25, 28, 40, 45, 52, 58, 60, 64, 66, 67, 70, 80, 81–82
Lettera Rarissima (Columbus), 63, 72
The Life of Christopher Columbus by His Son Fernando (F. Columbus), 11–13
Lives (Plutarch), 22

McNeill, William, 79–80
A Map of the World . . . (Waldseemüller), 74–75
Marchena, Friar, 13, 18
Margarit, Pedro, 51, 56–58
Martins, Fernâo, 24–25
Martyr, Peter, 73, 75
massacre at La Navidad, 50–51
Medinaceli, count of, 18
Moniz Perestrello, Doña Felipa (wife of Columbus), 11, 13

Nash, Philip Tajitsu, 82
native Americans
  genocide of, 80
  impact of Columbus on, 7–8, 81–82
  as slaves, 56, 70
Natural History (Pliny), 22
New York Times Magazine, 86
Niña, 20, 31, 59
Norsemen, North American landing, 26
The Northmen, Columbus, and Cabot, 985–1503 (Bourne, ed.), 18, 40, 41, 63

On Architecture (Vitruvius), 21
On Marvelous Things (Aristotle), 26
Ovando, Nicolás de, 70

Pérez, Friar, 15
Pérez, Juan, 19
Petrarch, Francesco, 21
Pinta, 20, 31, 34, 40
Pinzón, Martin Alonso, 20, 31, 33, 37
  hunt for gold, 40, 42–43
Pinzón, Vicente Yañez, 20, 31, 37
Piscataway people, 85

Pius II, Pope, 22
Pizarro, Francisco, 84
Pliny, 22
Plutarch, 22
Polo, Marco, 15, 22, 24, 28
potato, significance of, 79–80
Prescott, William H., 77
Ptolemy, Claudius, 21–22, 23

quadrant, 29, 32
Quintanilla, Alfonso de, 15

Ramon, Padre, 78
Reconquista (Reconquest), 15
Redwing, Billy, 85
Renaissance, 21
Rethinking Columbus, 82, 85
"Rethinking Terminology"
    (Nash and Ireland), 82
Roldán, Francisco, 65–67, 71
Rustichello, 24

Sagan, Carl, 28
Sale, Kirkpatrick, 22, 46, 76, 81
San Salvador (Guanahaní), 35
Santa Maria, 20, 31
    wrecked, 41, 43
Santángel, Luis de, 17
Santo Domingo, 61–62, 65,
    68, 72
Shape of the World (d'Ailly), 22
slavery
    of blacks, 84–87
    of native Americans, 56, 70,
        84–87
smallpox, as biggest killer, 83
Soto, Hernando de, 84
syphilis, 49

Taínos, 37, 42, 59, 86
    extinction of, 81
    as trespassers, 68
Talavara commission, 14

Torres, Antonio de, 57
Torres, Luis de, 39
Toscanelli, Paolo, 24–27
Travels (Polo), 22
Treaty of Tordesillas, 57
Triana, Rodrigo de, 34

Vespucci, Amerigo, 68, 73–75
Vitruvius, 21
*The Voyage and Ordeal of Sir
    John Mandeville,* 28–29

Waldseemüller, Martin,
    74–75
    A Map of the World . . . ,
        74–75
Wauja people, 82
Weatherford, Jack, 85–87
Wilford, John Noble, 29, 86

Picture Credits

About the Author

Daniel C. Scavone grew up in Chicago, Illinois. He holds a Ph.D. and is a professor of ancient and modern history at the University of Southern Indiana in Evansville. He has been awarded three National Endowment for the Humanities fellowships.